A Tour of Honolulu
— IN THE EARLY 1840'S —

Gorham D. Gilman

WITH ANNOTATIONS BY GARY R. COOVER

Rollston Press

A Tour of Honolulu in the Early 1840's
by Gorham D. Gilman
Annotated by Gary R. Coover

All rights reserved. No part of this book may be reproduced, scanned, transmitted, or distributed in any printed or form electronic without the prior permission of the author except in the case of brief quotations embodied in articles or reviews.

Copyright © 2023 Rollston Press

ISBN-13: 978-1-953208-12-5

All images are in the public domain.

Cover Photo: Map of Honolulu enclosed in a letter from Richard Charlton dated August 25, 1843. Located in the Public Record Office, London, (Foreign Office 115, Vo. 82) with subsequent annotations by A. Simpson.

Also by Gary R. Coover:

> *Honolulu Chinatown: 200 Years of Red Lanterns & Red Lights* (2022)
>
> *Pocket Walking Tour of Honolulu's Chinatown* (2023)
>
> *Downtown Honolulu's Lost Buildings and Forgotten Architects* (2023)
>
> *Honolulu 1854: The Drawings of Paul Emmert* (2023)

ROLLSTON PRESS
1717 Ala Wai Blvd #1703
Honolulu, HI 96815
USA
www.rollstonpress.com

Preface

With all the tall high-rise buildings now in downtown Honolulu, it is close to impossible to imagine what the city looked like in its very early days nearly 200 years ago.

Luckily for us today, late in his life at 80 years of age, Honolulu businessman Gorham D. Gilman recorded his reminiscences of Honolulu in the early 1840's, mentally strolling down each street and noting and commenting on the buildings and relating relevant stories.

Through Gilman's remembrances, the reader will be able to strip away the new buildings of today and travel back in time along the dusty roads to see and experience the early days of the city as it was transitioning from a sleepy little fishing village into the major business center in the middle of the Pacific Ocean.

First published in Thomas G. Thrum's *Hawaiian Almanac and Annual for 1904* as "Streets of Honolulu in the Early Forties" by Gorham D. Gilman, the text presented here is exactly as originally spelled and punctuated, complete, word for word – with only occasional subject headings and extra paragraph breaks inserted for better readability. Additional writings of Gilman have been added from contemporary newspaper sources.

Maps and sketches and photographs from times shortly after Gilman's comments are added to bring additional life to his narrative. A brief biography of the author is also included.

Although originally written some 60 years after he first landed in Honolulu, subsequent historical research has shown Gilman's memory and observations to be incredibly accurate.

Not directly connected with Gilman, but certainly from the same time period, *Reminiscences of John Cook: Kamaaina and Forty-Niner*, first published in 1927, is included as an Appendix.

Gary R. Coover
Editor/Publisher
Rollston Press

Table of Contents

Streets of Honolulu in the Early Forties 5
    Nuʻuanu Street 8
    Kaʻahumanu Street 13
    Merchant Street 14
    Queen Street 19
    Fort Street 25
    Union Street 32
    Hotel Street 33
    Richards Street 37
    Punchbowl Street 40
    King Street 41
    Palace Square 47
    Beretania Street 52
    Kawaiahao Church 58
    In Conclusion 60
Impressions of Honolulu, Past and Present 61
A Half Century Gone 68
Excerpt from Infancy of Honolulu 72
Gorham D. Gilman 74
Appendix: *Reminiscences of John Cook* 79
Acknowledgements & Thanks 106
Index 107

Streets of Honolulu in the Early Forties

In the spring of 1841 I had left the brig in which I had come around Cape Horn, as an occupant of the forecastle rather than the cabin, and at Valparaiso joined the good ship Gloucester from Boston, with the privilege of working my passage to Honolulu.

We had on board a large reinforcement of missionaries of the A. B. C. F. M. on their way to the islands, among them the Rev. Daniel Dole and wife, the father of the present Governor and the first principal of Punahou School (now Oahu College); Mr. Rice, whose widowed lady still lives to see the great changes wrought by her companions; the Rev, J. D. Paris and wife, who is at present represented by his son, a senator, and his daughter, the poetess; Rev. Elias Bond and wife, and others.

After a pleasant but uneventful voyage, the ship rounded Diamond Head just at sunset, giving us our first glimpse of the tropic scenery back of the city of Honolulu, but too late to enter the port before night, so the ship was laid "off and on" until the morning, when the early hours saw us standing in for the entrance to the port.

Honolulu Harbor, November 1840 (J.D. Dana)

Half way between Diamond Head and the harbor the pilot boat met us, the first revelation to the many on board of the Hawaiian, in his native simplicity, I might almost say, for in the freshness of the breeze and the flying spray, the men had doffed their foreign garments, and their brown skins glistened with the water which flew over them and their whale boat.

I can recall, even at this distant time, the profound impression made upon two of the missionary ladies, one of whom was Mrs. Dole, by their first sight of the natives among whom they were to pass their lives. It was with an evident feeling of depression that they retired to their cabin.

Not the least unique figure was that of the pilot himself, Mr. Stephen Reynolds, who with his broad brimmed Panama hat and white cotton shirt, with an ample collar, and a pair of nankeen trousers without suspenders endeavoring to keep his balance in the unsteady boat until he was safely alongside and on board.

The anchor down and the sails furled, the passengers made ready for landing. A large sixteen oared boat belonging to the governor had been obtained to take the missionary party onshore.

My position as sailor gave me the place of bow oar in Capt. Easterbrook's gig, manned by five men. We had as our passengers, the Captain and the supercargo, Mr. William Hooper, of the firm of Brinsmade, Ladd & Co., who was afterwards American consul.

It was a long pull, and a steady race between the two boats as to which should be the first to reach the shore. The boys in the gig were successful and I had the pleasure of throwing my bow oar onto the little landing place at the foot of Nuuanu street, thus winning the race.

Honolulu Harbor (Paul Emmert, 1854)

QUEEN STREET

What is now known as Queen street was then only a pathway along the water's edge, the water coming up most of the way between what are now Nuuanu and Kaahumanu streets.

Along the mauka side of the street was a collection of straw houses with lanais. There was not a frame building at this time in this distance between the two streets.

On the Ewa side of Nuuanu street stood the building occupied by B. L. & Co. in which was also the consul's office, where I was to be domesticated as the youngest clerk of the establishment, and which was my business home for some years. Besides my duties as clerk I performed some services for the consul.

Makai of the store was a small wharf built by B. L. & Co. standing out into deep water so that a vessel could load alongside or discharge its cargo.

Honolulu Harbor (Edward T. Perkins, 1854)
From *Na Motu; or Reef-Rovings in the South Seas*

Well on in the direction of Ewa there were the premises of the old Manini family and beyond them the Nuuanu stream.

NUʻUANU STREET

Coming back to Nuuanu street and passing mauka, I had my first glimpse of the Hawaiian maiden. She was coming down the street barefooted, and with only a *mumu* for a garment. I do not doubt that she was as curious to see the strange white boy as he was to see her.

On the left hand side of the street stood the store of the old gentleman, familiarly known as "old Grimes," an American who had been for very many years a resident of the place. His store was filled with a varied assortment of goods for trading with the natives.

E. & H. GRIMES,
COMMISSION MERCHANTS
AND DEALERS IN
GENERAL MERCHANDISE,
Eliab Grimes,
Hiram Grimes.
HONOLULU, OAHU, H. I.

His wife was a native woman, and she had a brother whose name was Manuahi, who was permitted to be a salesman behind the counter. Naturally feeling favorably inclined towards his countrymen and women, he was the favorite clerk with the customers of the establishment, for when selling goods, and particularly measuring off dry goods, he was often requested by the buyer to slip his scissors further along than the exact measure, thus giving sometimes quite a large extra piece. This custom caused the use of his name all over the islands as a synonym for an over measure in the way of trade.

Going mauka, (the latter word means in the native language *from the sea*, or mountainward, as its companion word, makai, means *toward the sea*, so that they may be used anywhere on the islands), we come next on the left hand side of Nuuanu street to the large lot occupied by the Hudson Bay Company, surrounded by a high stone wall.

The offices of the Company were in a two story wooden building with the end and entrance on the street. The agent was Mr. George Pelly, an Englishman of the Englishmen, associating very little with the people of the town, as in his opinion became a representative of the great Hudson Bay Company.

GEORGE PELLY & GEORGE T. ALLAN,
AGENTS FOR THE
HUDSON'S BAY COMPANY,
HONOLULU, OAHU, H. I.

The lot next mauka brings us to the corner of Nuuanu and King streets. My recollection is that King street did not receive its distinctive name till some time later than that of which I am writing. Quite a number of the streets waited several years after they were laid out before they received names, and it would be hard to tell now who named them. Like Topsy, "they just growed."

On the corner of the street alluded to was the well known saloon of Joe Booth, a typical Englishman of the opposite character from his adjoining neighbor, Mr. Pelly. Joe, as he was familiarly called by almost everybody, was famous for his large hospitality to all sailors visiting the port, and the "Blonde" was a favorite resort because of the genial characteristics of its host. From the tall flagstaff at the corner of the street floated the flag of Merrie England, and no more patriotic representative of his country lived in town.

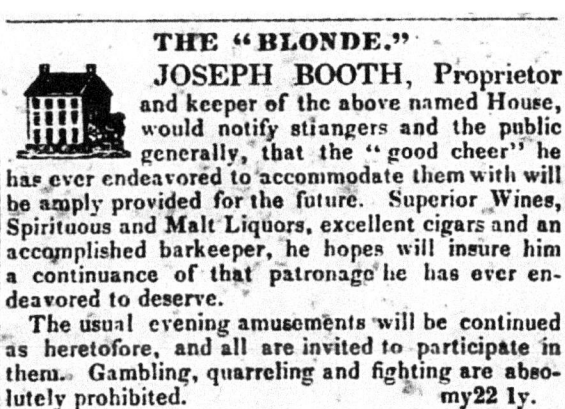

THE "BLONDE."
JOSEPH BOOTH, Proprietor and keeper of the above named House, would notify strangers and the public generally, that the "good cheer" he has ever endeavored to accommodate them with will be amply provided for the future. Superior Wines, Spirituous and Malt Liquors, excellent cigars and an accomplished barkeeper, he hopes will insure him a continuance of that patronage he has ever endeavored to deserve.

The usual evening amusements will be continued as heretofore, and all are invited to participate in them. Gambling, quarreling and fighting are absolutely prohibited.   my22 ly.

Crossing Nuuanu street and passing on the left a row of native houses and lanais or open spaces, we come to the corner of Hotel street, where stood a building occupied as a store by a Chinaman.

It was also said to contain rooms for the benefit of those of his countrymen who were addicted to the use of opium. At that time, comparatively few of the natives or foreigners indulged in the drug, but it was said that occasionally some of the gentlemen from Bohemia "hit the pipe" in the bunks of the Chinaman.

On the opposite side of the street, a building was put up by the merchants of the town for a somewhat singular purpose. There had come to Honolulu from Australia a couple of enterprising young men who had established themselves in business in the small one story house cornering on Hotel and Nuuanu streets. They had opened a store with a very small variety of dry goods, mostly common cotton cloth and stockings. Up to their arrival, most dry goods were sold at the rate of so many yards for a dollar. If silk, it might be one yard, calico might be two or three yards, cotton cloth, four yards for a dollar, the uniform prices observed by all merchants.

These enterprising Englishmen, not having a great variety to offer, and wishing to draw custom, announced to the native buyers that they would sell six yards of cloth for a dollar, and a pair of stockings for twenty-five cents, instead of the usual price of fifty. No doubt these prices paid them well, and as trade increased were obliged to purchase a larger variety of dry goods to add to their stock, and acted on the principle that "a nimble sixpence was worth more than a dull shilling."

As their trade increased proportionately, a meeting of the merchants was called to see what measures could be taken to crowd these interfering young men out of business. It was resolved to build a store on the right hand side of Nuuanu street, diagonally across from the new comers, and to endeavor to check their rapidly growing popularity by underselling them. An agreement having been made by all the merchants that they would not from that time furnish them with any more goods, they expected to be able to compel them either to come to the old rates or go out of business. The merchants counted without their host.

As is generally the case, there was some one who was not true to the agreement, commonly suspected by the rest to be a fellow countryman on King street, who was more anxious for a little profit than for his reputation, and so the game of opposition did not last long.

assing Hotel street there were scarcely any houses except a few of the natives, until we come to Beretania street.

On the corner of Nuuanu and Chapel streets, was one of the most pretentious mansions in the town built of coral stone, handsomely joined, "with wide verandas facing the beautiful Nuuanu valley. This was occupied by Mr. Skinner, an English gentleman engaged in merchandising.

Skinner House (Paul Emmert, 1854)

As it comes to my recollection, after these many years, Mr. Skinner's family was an illustration of the general condition of the intercourse between the English and American residents. There was comparatively little social interchange. Of course it was not ostracism, but except on special occasions they seldom mingled.

I may say, that this condition of society was very markedly indicated when a few years later the Islands were brought under the English flag. It was then made very evident that our friends from Britain felt their superiority, that the islands had come under British control, and that the Americans must take second. place.

Continuing our way up Nuuanu street we come to the corner of Beretania street, which will be as far mauka as we propose to go.

On the Waikiki side of this corner stood the residence of Dr. and Mrs. Rooke, who were the foster parents of Queen Emma. This residence was one of the most hospitable in town and the doctor's genial disposition made him many friends.

Dr. Rooke House

Emma, as she was usually called before the title of Queen was added to her name, was an exceedingly pleasant and agreeable young girl. She was an attendant at the Royal School where the children of the high chiefs were being educated for the positions which they were likely to assume in later life.

Dr. Thomas C.B. Rooke, Emma, Grace Kamaikui Young Rooke

KA'AHUMANU STREET

Returning to the water side, we will pass along the waterfront to the next short street – now known as Kaahumanu – running mauka from the water to what was afterwards known as Merchant street.

The space between this street and Nuuanu was mostly occupied by native straw houses with lanais in front of them and used principally as a fish market. The water of the harbor ebbed and flowed on the makai side of the street.

There were one or two low story shed like buildings on the Waikiki side of Kaahumanu street, which were afterwards utilized as stores.

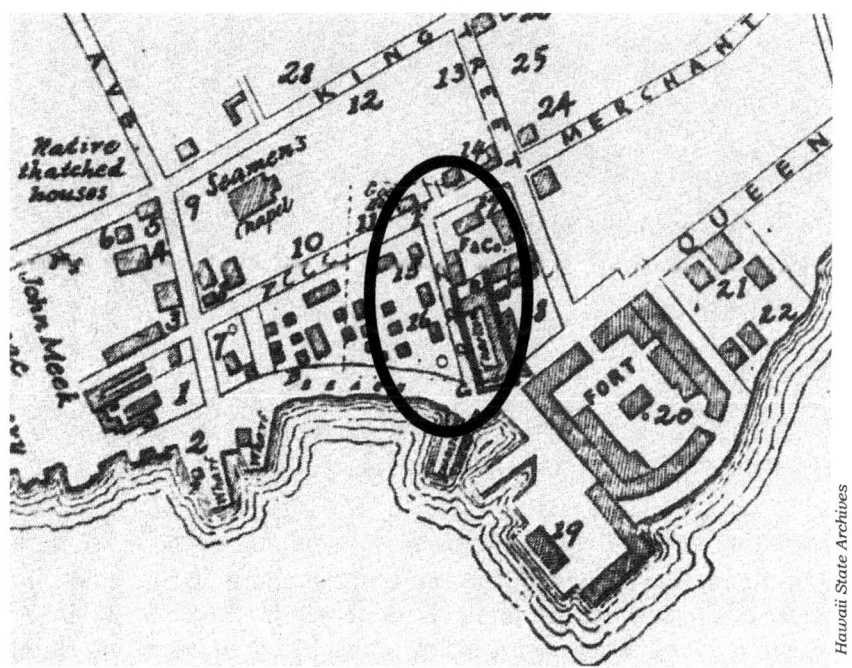

Ka'ahumanu Street (Charlton Map, 1843)

MERCHANT STREET

The next street mauka, running parallel with the harbor front from Nuuanu to Fort, (beyond Fort street this street was not much more than a mere lane which ran out to the large open space in front of the palace, there uniting with King street,) is now known as Merchant street.

Stephen Reynolds Store (Paul Emmert, 1854)

On the mauka corner of Nuuanu and Merchant streets stood the store of one of the most noted characters of the town, Mr. Stephen Reynolds, originally from Boxford, Mass. He had been very many years at the islands, and was one of the most remarkable men in Honolulu.

He was very peculiar in his dress as well as his thinking. His clothes were cut in his own fashion, generally what we know as the jacket and trousers and made of light colored nankeen.

His shirt was always of unbleached cotton cloth, destitute of any linen bosom, buttoned in front at the throat with a wide turned over collar, white stockings and low shoes, and a Panama hat destitute of any ribbon completed his costume.

Stephen Reynolds
Courtesy Hawaiian Historical Society

This style I do not recall ever to have seen changed. The simplicity of the costume was somewhat characteristic of the man.

A visitor to his store went up the half dozen well worn planks to the somewhat rickety veranda and entering within found a most miscellaneous assortment of dry goods and notions in what would be to him an indescribable confusion, yet the kindly gentleman, past middle life, with a. very pleasant manner to his native customers, found no difficulty in meeting their wishes. and enjoyed a large share of their confidence.

It was not, however, so much as a merchant that he impressed himself upon the community, but as a man of mental ability.

Naturally a student, with an evident predilection for the study of the law, he was, in the absence of any educated attorney residing in the town, the person who was generally consulted on matters that were coming before the courts.

In two most important cases which I recall, one the trial of Mr. L. L. Torbert, and the other the celebrated case of Messrs. Ladd & Co. against the government, which forms a part of the history of those times, Mr. Reynolds was engaged as principal attorney for Ladd & Co., and his conduct of these cases was considered very remarkable for an unprofessional man.

I may add here that the kindness of Mr. Reynolds' heart was shown in later years by his establishing a home for young Hawaiian girls, where he gave them the best education which could be provided for them.

On the makai side of the road (now Merchant street), from Nuuanu to Kaahumanu street, were empty lots, with blocks of coral for fences.

The next building on the mauka side was the store of Messrs. John and William Paty, a two story building, the second story being used for offices.

Capt. John Paty and Mr. William Paty were brothers from Plymouth, Mass. The captain had an enviable reputation as captain of the bark Don Quixote, the regular packet plying between Honolulu and San Francisco.

Some years later he was complimented with a blue silk commodore's flag with the figures 100 in white upon it. indicative of his one hundreth passage made between the coast and the islands.

Mr. William, the brother, had charge of the general merchandise store, which stood at the head of Kaahumanu street.

Capt. John H. Paty

The descendants of Mr. and Mrs. William Paty are the well known family of the Mott-Smiths. A little incident is worth relating here. The first time that a sufficient number of ladies could be gathered together to form two sets for dancing was in the home of Mr. and Mrs. William Paty, on Beretania street.

Continuing our walk along Merchant street, on the mauka side, the next was a wooden building of two stories with a lookout upon the top. It was generally used by the public whenever the cry of "Sail ho!" rang through the streets.

Honolulu Hale (Paul Emmert, 1854)

Near the corner of Merchant and Fort streets, mauka side, was a small one story building which was later destroyed to give place to a fine stone building erected by Capt. Snow, a ship master who had followed the trade between Boston and Honolulu and retired and entered into general business.

Makee & Anthon (B.F. Snow) Building, (Paul Emmert, 1854)

On the makai side of the street, were the premises of Mr. William French. These extended from Kaahumanu to Fort street, surrounded by a high picket fence with some noble hau trees standing just within the line of the fence.

The building was quite a sizeable one of wood, with a high basement and large trading rooms above.

Building on the French Premises (Paul Emmert, 1854)

Mr. French was one of the oldest residents and a person of considerable influence. The house was better known a little later as that of French and Greenway.

QUEEN STREET

Before describing Fort street we will take a look at the famous premises of James Robinson & Co., at that time the only ship builders and repairers on the islands and in fact in the Pacific.

It was a rather peculiar partnership in the make up of the firm which began in 1822, though the shipyard at the point, "Pakaka," was not established till 1827.

The firm comprised Jas. Robinson, Robt. Lawrence and Robt. Holt. The two former were together in the Hermes, which vessel with the Pearl, set forth from this port on a whaling cruise, and both ran ashore twenty days out on an unknown reef afterwards named for the lost vessels.

Mr. R. built a schooner from the wrecks in which with eleven others he reached these islands in Oct. 1822. This vessel was the foundation of their subsequent business and fortune.

Robinson Warehouse (Paul Emmert, 1854)

Mr. Robinson, the senior of the firm, was considered a ship carpenter of skill and ability; Mr. Lawrence, familiarly called "Bobby," was the book-keeper, house keeper, and general steward of the establishment. Some of his boarders, all men, used to remark that the bread which he made occasionally tasted of the oakum which he was in the constant habit of picking from bits of tarred rope which he carried in his pocket.

Mr. Holt was an American and much the best equipped for managing the business of the partners.

They occupied for their headquarters a two-story stone building under the walls of the old fort, the lower part unoccupied except for storage, the upper part used as office and living apartments.

At the time of the death of the last surviving partner, Mr. James V. Austin, who was their attorney, went into the lower part and, guided by some directions, unearthed a large amount of coin which had been secretly and safely buried there.

Proceeding along Queen street on the makai side, we come to the old fort. This is so historically well known that it needs no description from me. Its walls extended along the street to some distance past Fort street, at the foot of which the large gateway served for entrance and exit.

Honolulu Fort (Paul Emmert, 1854)
Courtesy Hawaiian Historical Society

Over this gateway on two occasions were erected scaffolds for the execution of two couples, men and women, for having committed murder. Indicative of the natives' superstition was an incident connected with the last execution.

The streets near and approaching the fort were packed with natives, men and women, who had come from all parts of the island to witness the execution. They had waited as patiently as could be expected for the appearance of the criminals, but the moment that the drop fell, and it was evident that they had paid the penalty of their crime with their lives, the people as if actuated by one common thought, cried out "Ghosts, Ghosts," and ran like a flock of frightened sheep in the opposite direction as fast as their legs could carry them, and in a short space of time the streets were cleared.

On the mauka side of the street, on the corner of Kaahumanu, was the store of the firm of Henry Skinner & Co., English merchants who figured quite conspicuously two or three years later in the events of Lord George Paulet's seizure of the islands.

The junior member of the firm, who was commonly called Bobby Robeson, was said to have put in a claim against the government for the sum of "three thousand dollars for personal injuries." It was commonly reported at the time that the "injuries" were the result of an altercation which he had with his washerwoman, and that she got the better of him.

Interior of the Fort (Paul Emmert, 1854)
Courtesy Hawaiian Historical Society

There is connected with the old fort a national incident which, although I have referred to it in a previous article, may not be amiss here.

It was on the occasion of the cession of the islands and government, forced by the acting English consul Alexander Simpson, and Lord George Paulet, an apparently willing tool in the hands of the much more able British consul.

The day and hour for the cession had come. The king and his chiefs with Dr. G. P. Judd as the official interpreter, stood on one part of the veranda of the governor's house overlooking the large area of the fort and a little distance ahead from them on the same veranda, though evidently nearer than the royal party desired, and without any interchange of courtesies other than the most formal, were Lord George, the acting English consul and a few officers.

Below on the parade ground were a detachment of the Hawaiian troops and also a little distance from them the British soldiers from H. B. M. Frigate Carysfort.

The time having arrived, the king stepped to the front of the platform, which was a signal for quiet from the small number who had gathered to witness the painful ceremony.

The American party refused to be witnesses on the occasion, while some of the English residents did not attempt to conceal their satisfaction that the islands were to pass under the English flag.

Lord George Paulet

It was then that the king gave utterance with faltering voice to the words spoken in Hawaiian. "The life of the land has gone."

The remainder of the brief speech is a matter of record. The official papers were then read by Dr. Judd, and at a given signal a national salute was fired, the Hawaiian flag was lowered, the English flag was raised, and a national salute paid to it.

The ceremony being over, the English troops left the fort with the band playing "Isle of Beauty, fare thee well," which was felt by many of the old residents as a needless insult added to injury.

On the Waikiki side of the fort was a short street running from Queen street to the water. Near Queen street was Halekauwila, one of the largest and finest thatched houses on the island, the town residence of the king and queen and also at times the place of meeting of the council.

Makai at the water's edge, was a small cottage of plastered adobe, with a veranda extending all around it, called Mauna Kilika, also used for government purposes, and later by the English Admiral Thomas who came to the islands to restore the flag and the government to the rightful authorities.

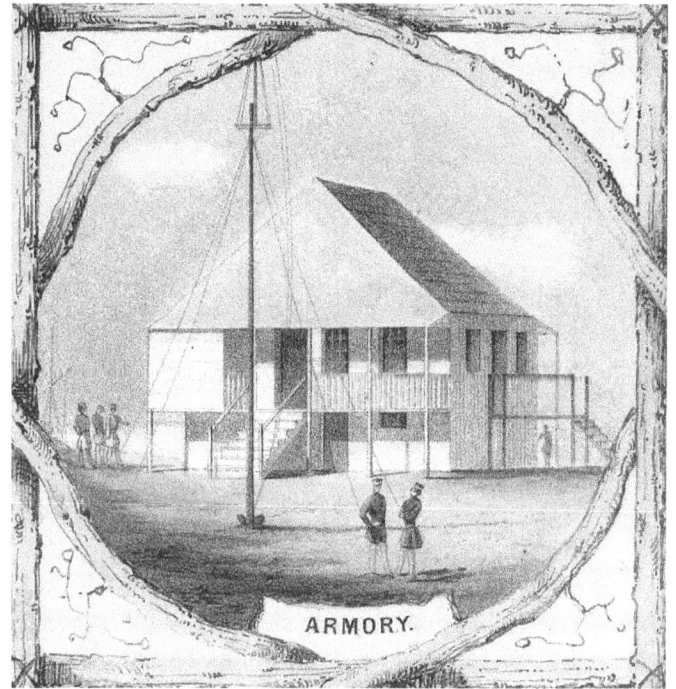

Mauna Kilika (Paul Emmert, 1854)

Beyond this towards Waikiki were the premises occupied by Governor Kekuanoa and beyond these the residence of the high chiefess Kekauonohi and her husband, Kealiiahonui, son of the former king of Kauai, who was brought as a hostage from that island and married to his royal companion.

These were the only buildings of any importance on the whole length of the street from Fort street to the mission premises, with the single exception of the Oahu Charity School, a coral building which was erected for the education of the half white children of the place.

Oahu Charity School (Paul Emmert, 1854)

This school was conducted by Mr. A. Johnstone, whose square two story resilience stood the last house on the mauka side of King street before coming to the plains, called Kulaokahua. I think that the present residence of Mr. C. H. Atherton occupies the spot where Mr. Johnstone's house stood.

Beyond this the plain stretched from the slopes of Punchbowl to the sea, broken only by two residences, one called Makiki, with its little grove of hau trees, the only green spot on the extensive plain. One other place seaward was called Little Britain, residence of the late J. N. Wright.

FORT STREET

Coming again to Fort street and going mauka, the first building was on the Waikiki corner of Fort and Merchant, where Mr. John Cummins had a store.

Mauka was the only Chinese bakery managed by Sam Sing & Co., on the site of Lewers & Cooke's late store.

Adjoining on the corner of King street was a story and a half building used as a store, later occupied by E. O. Hall. On the Ewa side of the street there were only native buildings with an adobe fence in front.

Proceeding mauka on the same side, was a small adobe building near Hotel street occupied by Mr. E. C. Webster, as a dry goods store.

An amusing incident connected with this gentleman may be worth relating. Standing by the gateway in front of his store, early one morning he was accosted by Admiral Thomas, who looking up at the sign and seeing the name Webster, asked him if he was any relation to the great Daniel Webster, to which he quickly replied, "Yes sir, I am his grandfather."

The Admiral apparently appreciated the humor of the situation, as Mr. Webster was a smaller man than the average, scarcely weighing a hundred pounds, but though diminutive in size, he had an active brain and made himself felt on several occasions by his ability in legal matters, and in connection with Mr. Reynolds formerly alluded to conducted several very important cases.

On the opposite side of the street were the premises of Pierce & Brewer. Their building was quite retired from the street and their large premises were occupied by store houses.

This firm were the successors to James L. Hunnewell, who was an officer on board the brig Thaddeus, that carried the first missionaries from Boston to the islands, and who afterwards returned to the islands and entered into a very successful business career.

C.Brewer, S.H. William (Paul Emmert, 1854)

There was but one more building on the same side of the street, and that was located on the corner of Fort and Hotel, occupied by the dry goods store of Robert Davis, a native of Honolulu, half white, finely educated in the United States, and afterwards Judge of the Police Court.

Crossing Hotel street mauka, on the right hand side was a small building, the first occupant of which, I do not recall, but subsequently Dr. Mott-Smith and Dr. Hildebrand were located herewith an apothecary store on the lower floor and a dentist office above.

The next premises was quite a large building of two stories, plastered adobe, and known as the French Hotel.

French Hotel (Paul Emmert, 1854)

Next mauka, were the premises occupied by Capt. John O. Dominis, father of the late Governor Dominis, who lived there until Washington Place was built. After Mr. Dominis had moved, the place was occupied by the American consul, Mr. Terrill.

Dominis House (Paul Emmert, 1854)

Then came the premises now known as the Sister's School and then the Roman Catholic church.

Catholic Church (Paul Emmert, 1854)

Brewer House, Catholic Church (Lydia Nye, 1843)
Courtesy Hawaiian Historical Society

And about this time, on the corner of Beretania street and Fort, was built the large residence of Mr. Charles Brewer.

Brewer House (Paul Emmert, 1854)

I recall distinctly, at this period, the planting of the hau trees along the sides of the roads. They were cut up in the mountains, some ten or twelve feet long, destitute of any branches, and the trunks were about the thickness of a man's arm. These were stuck in the ground, and the earth filled in around them.

To what size they may have grown since then your reader can tell better than I. (The last succumbed with the erection of the McIntyre Building. – Ed.)

On the Ewa side of Fort street on the corner of Hotel stood the dwelling house of Mr. John Colcord, a blacksmith by trade, a very worthy man.

There were no other buildings of note that I remember on this side of the street until we came to a somewhat narrow lane extending from Fort street to Nuuanu, and about midway of this lane on the makai side, was the cottage of the well known Father Damon, the seaman's chaplain of the port.

Reverend Damon House (Paul Emmert, 1854)

Few men of that time were more respected by the seamen and landsmen than was the chaplain. He officiated on Sunday at the Bethel to the small congregation that attended the services during the off seasons.

During the time that the whale ships were in port the room was generally well filled with sailors from the ships.

Speaking of the chapel reminds me of an incident that occurred there which caused me some embarrassment.

A ship had arrived in port for wood and water with a large number of Mormon emigrants, under the leadership of the afterwards famous Sam Brannan of San Francisco notoriety. An evening meeting was announced, at which the said Brannan acting as a Mormon elder presided. I had in some way become possessed with the idea that these Mormons had been recruited from the Methodist denomination.

During one of the pauses in the service, I started to sing to a familiar "Pennyroyal meter" as it used to be called at home, the well-known hymn, "When I can read my title clear," with the Pennyroyal variations, "and wipe my weeping eyes." Two or three voices in the crowded room essayed to help, but left me on the second verse to finish it alone.

Not willing to acknowledge defeat, I started the third verse, which I had to sing entirely as a solo. As I could not read a note of music and sang only by ear, remembering only the old fashioned peculiarities of the tune, my effort was not a success.

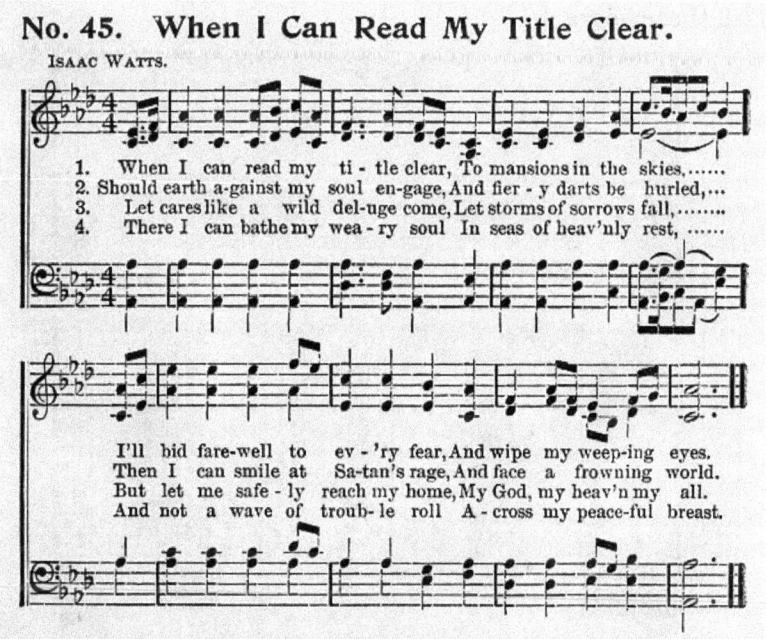

UNION STREET

Branching off from Fort street as we go mauka, there was a bit of road extending its somewhat crooked way from Hotel street to Beretania street.

On its left-hand side was a long two-story coral building in which Dr. R. W. Wood had his office. In the upper story, it might have been a few years later, Capt. Newell and his family resided. Capt. Newell will be remembered by the residents of a little later period as the commander of the vessel which bore away from the islands to China, Hon. George Brown, United States Commissioner, who had ceased to be "persona grata" to the Hawaiian government, and also the well known and popular Capt. John Dominis.

The vessel and her passengers were never heard from after sailing. It was generally supposed that she was wrecked in one of the fierce typhoons of the China seas, though for many years the devoted wife and mother was ever expecting to hear of the rescue of her beloved husband.

On the Waikiki side of the street and mauka of where the only engine house in the city stood was the residence of Mrs. Dowsett, whose well known family have been prominent in Honolulu affairs for all these years.

Mrs. Dowsett House (Paul Emmert, 1854)

HOTEL STREET

Still further on the mauka side of Hotel street we come to the famous Adams' premises, which the old gentleman occupied with his numerous descendants.

Beyond these, still towards Waikiki, was a little single cottage of Mr. George Pelly, agent of the Hudson Bay Company. The high stone wall around the premises was considered indicative of the exclusiveness of this representative of the great company.

Directly mauka of these premises but in the "Adams' yard," as it was called, was the building occupied by the Odd Fellows, the first organization of this Order instituted in the North Pacific. I had the honor of being the first initiate and with William C. Parke of beloved memory, formed one of the charter members, giving it its name of Excelsior, anticipating what it might attain to, and which expectations seems to have been realized.

We come now to what is known as Alakea street. On the Ewa corner makai of this street was a fine large straw house which I remember at this time as the residence of Judge Robertson, a man well known and still remembered for his sterling worth and integrity of character.

On the Waikiki corner stood a two story stone house, occupied by Mr. James Jackson Jarves and his wife. He was the promoter of the effort at silk culture at Koloa. Kauai, which proved a failure for the lack of a sufficiently low temperature to allow the cocoons to come into the proper condition to produce silk. See Mr. Jarves' very full account in his book, "Scenes and Scenery of the Sandwich Islands."

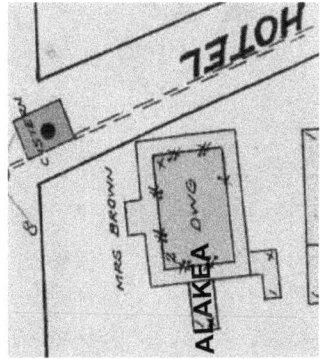

Dakin Map, 1899

James Jackson Jarves

Mr. Jarves was also at one time the editor of the weekly newspaper, called The Polynesian.

A startling announcement was made in one of its issues which caused no end of speculation and talk. It stated with a good deal of minuteness that "a young American had disappeared on the morning of the Fourth of July; when last seen he was entering the gates of the fort, since which time no trace of him had been found."

The secret leaked out before the next week's issue that Mr. Jarves had taken that day and occasion, for forswearing his own country, the United States, and had taken the oath of allegiance to His Majesty Kamehameha III.

[Before] Crossing the street and passing mauka on the left hand corner, stood the little cottage of Mr. William Wond, a somewhat noted saloon keeper of the better sort.

The little cottage had, however, another occupant whose name has become associated with the introduction of Odd Fellowship into the islands. Dr. Watson brought the first charter for a lodge of the Order and instituted Excelsior Lodge, which has proved itself worthy of its name, its course ever having been "onward and upward,"

I am recently informed by the senior officer of the Lodge that I am now the only one living of the original charter members. Sixty years is a long look backward. This building stood where the Honolulu Library now stands.

Honolulu Library and Reading Room (1883)

On the opposite Waikiki side of the street was erected a little later, perhaps, the first Hawaiian theatre.

There are those who well remember it and the scenes enacted therein. The establishment of this theatre was largely due to the efforts of a set of young amateurs, among whom was Charley Vincent, a well known carpenter, and Mr. J. H. Brown, a man about town, and later Captain of the Honolulu Guards and Police Chief.

Royal Hawaiian Theatre (c.1852-1881)

Royal Hawaiian Theatre (Paul Emmert, 1854)

One evening in particular was noted for the performance of the opera of "Martha," of which Kamehameha IV. was the stage manager, while Queen Emma and Mrs. Bernice P. Bishop and other noted ladies of society formed its chorus. The programs were printed upon white satin. There may possibly be some of these souvenirs still to be found in Honolulu.

Mauka of the theatre was the little cottage occupied by Mr. Charles R. Bishop and his young bride Bernice Pauahi Bishop.

Mauka of this was the quite large residence occupied by William French.

William French House (Paul Emmert, 1854)

Windmill at William French's House (Paul Emmert, 1854)

RICHARDS STREET

The next parallel street was Richards street. Makai of King street was erected by Mr. B. Shillaber, an American engaged in the China trade, "the Bungalow," something after the style of the East India houses, where there was a general dispensation of bachelor hospitality.

The Bungalow (Paul Emmert, 1854)

Mauka on the palace side of the street was a series of low one-story buildings occupied at different times by the Princess Victoria and her brother, Prince Lot, Kamehameha V.

Prince Victoria and Prince Lot House (Paul Emmert, 1854)

Next mauka were the old premises of the Sumner family of which your courts have heard not a little in the last few months.

William Sumner House (Paul Emmert, 1854)

Still mauka crossing a narrow lane, afterwards designated as Palace Walk, came a large open ground in which was the residence of Haalelea.

And mauka of this, coming up to Beretania street, was the residence of Kaeo, and Lahilahi, the parents of the late Prince Albert recently deceased. The Central Union church now covers the ground formerly occupied by these houses.

Adjoining, on Beretania street, was the residence of the French consul, Jules Dudoit, in whose family were also Mrs. and Miss Corney, his wife's mother and sister; premises subsequently occupied for many years by Jas. Smith of land office memory.

From this place the consul and his family moved in 1845, to their newly completed mansion on the opposite side of the same street, near Fort, known of late years as the Dickson premises.

Dudoit House on Beretania (Paul Emmert, 1854)

Mons. Dudoit had the reputation of being, among other things, a caricaturist, and often highly amused the merchants of the water front with his timely hits.

PUNCHBOWL STREET

The next and last street running parallel was that known as Punchbowl street.

There was on the entire length of this street, from the makai side to the slopes of Punchbowl, but one residence, the two-story house, built of coral, of Mr. Henry Dimond, mauka of King street.

Beyond the street was the old Kawaiahao church and burying ground. A more forsaken, desolate-looking place than the latter can scarcely be imagined. One to see it in its present attractiveness of fences, trees and shrubbery, can hardly believe its former desolation, when without enclosure, horses and cattle had free access to the whole space. The transformation was mainly owing to the labors of Mrs. Armstrong, wife of the missionary, who was pastor at one time of the Church.

The houses of "The Mission" I had better leave to be described by some of the children whose homes were there.

Mission Houses on left with Dimond House at back center (Daniel Wheeler, 1837)

Having now taken up the description of the streets running from the makai side of the town mauka, and also having mentioned Queen and Merchant streets running at right angles to the others, we will now turn to the three remaining parallel streets, namely King, Hotel, and Beretania.

King Street

Beginning at the Nuuanu stream end of King street there were a few scattering native houses near the river side.

The first house that we notice was a store kept by Isaac Montgomery, a true son of the Emerald Isle. He had been fortunate in business and had a fair financial standing. It was generally believed that the temptations of ready money, a quick sale even at small profit. induced him to supply the enterprising Australians with goods desirable to keep up their trade.

ISAAC MONTGOMERY,
DEALER IN GENERAL MERCHANDISE,
HONOLULU, OAHU, H. I.
Ships supplied with Stock at the shortest notice.

On the same side of the street was a square medium-sized, plastered adobe house owned by Capt. John Meek. This was used as a lodge room for the new Masonic lodge, the first organized in Honolulu, if not in the Pacific, under the name of "Le Progres de l'Oceanie." This antedated somewhat the formation of the Odd Fellows' Lodge, and many of the business and professional men of the town were initiated as members. I hold a certificate in the handwriting of Liholiho, King Kamehameha IV., as Worshipful Master of the Lodge.

The next premises on that side of the street, as I remember, was occupied by natives and joined the premises of the Blonde, already mentioned.

On the mauka side of the street were the large grounds of Capt. John Meek, extending almost the entire length of the block to Nuuanu street. Capt. Meek was one of the noted characters of the place; a retired ship master who had settled in the islands years before and become possessed of large tracts of land and herds of cattle. He shared with Stephen Reynolds the duties of pilot.

Crossing Nuuanu street on the makai side were a row of native houses with lanais, used for a fish market.

The first principal building, and a conspicuous one, was the Seamen's Bethel. At the time of our arrival there was no stated occupant of the pulpit. Rev. Daniel Dole, who came with the reinforcement of missionaries was requested to take charge of the little congregation made up of foreign residents of different nationalities in the one place where it seemed possible to gather those who, though differing widely in politics and social amenities, met in this little upper room and united in divine worship.

The Seamen's Bethel (Paul Emmert, 1854)

A story was told which marks the estimation in which the British consul, Mr. Charlton, was held, to the effect that those interested in the service wanted a name for a new singing book which had been gotten together for the use of the congregation.

Among other names proposed was the "Honolulu Lyre," to which objection was made that we already had a notorious Honolulu liar, (referring to Charlton) and some other name was selected.

Not the least interesting part of the congregation was the gathering of the children, particularly of the members of the royal school, consisting of the four grandchildren of old Kamehameha, of whom three became kings, and also the families of Mr. and Mrs. Gulick and Mr. and Mrs. Emerson, names which have become noted in many lands for their missionary efforts.

These and other members of missionary families, (there were but very few children of the residents as distinguished from the missionaries), formed the majority of the Sabbath School, the only one in town taught in English.

There was no other conspicuous building on this side of the street up to Fort street; only some few native houses where fish and poi were sold.

Opposite the Bethel on the mauka side of the street was a one-story, white-plastered adobe building, standing end to the street, which was occupied as a tailor's shop by one C. H. Nicholson, a man of large size but finely proportioned, dressed immaculately in the finest of white linen, but to use a common expression, "as black as the ace of spades."

Charles H. Nicholson Shop (Paul Emmert, 1854)

When he and his Hawaiian wife, who matched him well in size, took their promenades they attracted general attention. The shop was the favorite rendezvous for the gossips of the village, who generally gathered there in the evening, to discuss the events of the day. This building had the same location which for so many years has been occupied by Castle & Cooke.

A little blind alley between high adobe walls led from King street to Hotel street coming out at Thompson's famous saloon, a man who although he kept a saloon told me that for years he did not know the taste of liquors.

Continuing in the direction of Waikiki, we come to the large premises of Hannah Holmes, or Mrs. Jones, as she was at one time the wife of the American consul.

At this time the house "was the most pretentious in the town, built of coral, with high basement and broad steps leading up to wide verandas; in the early times, a place of convivial hospitality.

Hannah Holmes House (Paul Emmert, 1854)

One day a native servant of Mrs. Holmes, who was herself a Hawaiian, came to the store where I was clerk and offered a single silver spoon for sale. The circumstances were so unusual that my employer, Mr. Ladd, sent me up to her house to see if she had authorized the sale, or whether the native had come improperly by it. Going to the house I met Mrs. Holmes with her son, afterwards Judge Robert Davis.

Not being at that time familiar with the Hawaiian language, and supposing that Mrs. Holmes did not understand English, I told my story to her son, who spoke perfectly correct English. Rather to my embarrassment he turned to his mother, and said in as good English as I had used, "Mother, you have heard this young man's story, what about the spoon?"

She replied in English, evidently understanding the language, having been three times married to Americans, "It is all right, I sent the spoon to be sold as I wanted a little money."

These premises were afterwards used as the Globe Hotel. Part of the grounds are now occupied by the Odd Fellows building on Fort street.

There was a singular little building at the corner of Fort and Hotel [King – Ed.] streets, which was almost an excrescence on the adjoining property and marred the line of the street. The owner was very averse to selling, and it remained for years an eyesore to all passers by.

Passing Fort street and beyond the corner now occupied by E. O. Hall & Son, Ltd., there was a long stretch of property occupied mostly by natives. *Alapai street had not yet been cut through, and the first house that I remember was that of Anton Silva, a Portuguese, an old resident, at the foot of Richard street, and at the junction of Merchant and King streets.

> • I am told that the street is now called Alakea street I am under the impression it was originally as I have written and so named in honor of John Young's wife, Alapai, a member of the king's court.

On the mauka Waikiki corner of King street and Fort were some native buildings which afterwards gave place to a wooden building erected for S. H. Williams for the disposition of his large stock of dry goods, in which store I was a clerk for sometime, afterwards McIntyre's bakery.

The next premises were the large property, well walled in, of the high chiefs, Paki and Konia, parents of Mrs. Pauahi Bishop. There was a fine large straw house with wide veranda, ample grounds, and a long row of servant's houses.

Paki's House (Paul Emmert, 1854)

One of the beautiful ornaments of the place was a fine large tamarind tree,* planted the day of Mrs. Bishop's birth.

* A section of the trunk is now in the Bishop Museum.

Next adjoining was the estate of Piikoi who was ranked with the hulumanus of the King. They were the personal attendants of His Majesty, the King, and wore the regalia of the famous yellow feather capes on occasions of state functions, hence their name.

From there out to Richards street there were no houses other than those occupied by natives.

Richards street, by the way, was not laid out as it now is, nor named until after the death of the Rev. William Richards for whom it was called.

PALACE SQUARE

We now come to the square occupied by the palace. This building was built of coral with a high basement and one story, high studded and sloping roof with a large lookout room on top. It was divided into a large hall through the centre, a large reception or throne room on the right, with two rooms on the left. It was mainly used for public purposes, the king preferring the quiet quarters of the cottages in the yard, where he lived according to his chosen Hawaiian style.

Some very brilliant receptions were held there to which the public was generally invited with all the official and distinguished guests who happened in town.

The First Royal Palace (Paul Emmert, 1854)

A little incident may not be out of place here. Having received an invitation to attend one of the receptions of King Kamehameha IV., a friend and myself entered the grounds at the mauka gate, intending to pass around and enter at the front of the building.

As we were passing the bungalow a friendly voice, somewhat familiar, hailed us and asked us to come upon the veranda. We accepted the invitation and were welcomed by the king himself, who invited us to seats and cigars.

While chatting upon social events the king, suddenly, looking at his watch, said hastily, "Excuse me, gentlemen, I am due in the throne room in five minutes," and disappeared within.

Passing to the front entrance of the palace, up the broad steps, and across the wide veranda to the brilliantly lighted rooms, we found a large company gathered.

In a short time the band announced the arrival of His Majesty and presentations began. These were made by the officers of the court, dressed in full uniform, and with great formality.

When our turn came, my friend Mr. Bartow, and myself were escorted by two of the officers to the presence of the king. We were announced with much formality by the stereotyped expression, "Your Majesty, permit me to present to you Mr. Gilman."

With a ·formal bow on the part of both, we passed on, as if it were the first time we had ever been in the royal presence, while really it was only a few minutes since we had been smoking together.

Kamehameha III

In earlier days, under the reign of Kamehameha III, an accommodating arrangement was made by which all of the missionary friends who desired were presented before the hour of nine o'clock, at which time the music struck up some lively tune, which was an indication that dancing was about to commence, and our good missionary friends understood the hint and retired.

A short distance from the palace was a two-story coral house, occupied by Kekauluohi and her husband Kanaina, who were the parents of Lunalilo, who afterwards came to the throne as William, the First.

There was one very modest building in the palace grounds, of very plain construction, without a window; the only light entering was through a heavy door which was the only opening. This was the tomb of the royal family, kings and·queens.

It was in this secluded retreat that Dr. G. P. Judd, King Kamehameha III's prime minister, found the only safe and quiet place in which he could enter his records of the passing events of the troublous times during Lord George Paulet's reign.

On the mauka borders of the palace property was the school building of the Young Chiefs' School, cared for and watched over by Mr. and Mrs. A. S. Cooke, formerly connected with the Mission.

The building was a one-story, plastered adobe building, surrounding an open court, with windows on the outside and the doors on the inside. It contained all the conveniences for housekeeping, school room, and dormitory in the one enclosure.

The Young Chief's School (Paul Emmert, 1854)

The school was organized for the purpose of educating properly the children of the high chiefs, who presumably would come to occupy the places of their parents who were active at the times of the second and third Kamehamehas.

The three oldest boys were the sons of Kinau and Gov. Kekuanoa. Although their children by birth, they had each of them been adopted, the youngest by Kamehameha III., the second, Lot, by the governor of Maui, the third and oldest, Moses, by the governor of Kauai.

Among the other younger boys were, David, afterwards Kalakaua, and his brother James, who died young, William Lunalilo, afterwards King, and two others, grandchildren of John Young. Among the girls, were Jane Loeau and Abigail Mahaha, from Kauai, Emma Rooke, who was afterwards the wife of Kamehameha IV., and Lydia Kamakaeha, the present ex-queen.

Also among the members of the school was the Princess Victoria, younger sister of the first three boys alluded to. With her were her two guardians, John Ii and his wife Sarai. Mr. Ii was one of the strongest men of the nation, a man of common birth, who by his own mental ability and absolute integrity had raised himself with his wife to the important position of the guardianship of the young princess, to whom the people looked with fond admiration, hoping that she might come to hold the exalted position of her mother, who was one of the rulers of the land, as the daughter of the old conquering king.

There was yet another scholar, Bernice Pauahi, the daughter of a long line of the most illustrious chiefs of the nation, and whose name and good deeds are linked imperishably, let us hope, with all that is high and noble in the educational interests of Hawaii.

Bernice Pauahi Bishop

The Kamehameha Schools are her monument, linked with the beneficence of her husband, the Hon. Charles R. Bishop, whom she made her choice, declining the offer of Kamehameha IV., and later, also, that of his brother who succeeded him, and later the throne of the kingdom, offered her on the death bed of King Kamehameha V.

They formed a very happy family of boys and girls, and appeared to enjoy their school life as much as any children in any boarding school on the mainland. They were under very careful and kind supervision by those who were their guardians and teachers, exhibited very favorable progress in their studies, and reflected much credit on their instructors.

An incident or two may be interesting connected with the three older boys. They were discussing together what they would do when they came into possession of the positions of their hereditary rank. The oldest, Moses, said, "When I am the governor of Kauai, I shall do so and so." Lot remarked. "When I am governor of Maui, having a larger population and more commerce, shall do so and so in the management of my affairs." Alexander, the youngest, and the heir apparent, said with a look of quiet assurance, "When you are governors, who will be king?"

The other incident was connected with the seizure of the islands by Lord George Paulet. Their teacher, Mr. Cooke, going into the room where the boys were, on the evening of that eventful day, found that they had cut off all of their government buttons from their jackets. Upon being asked why they had done such a thing, they replied, "We have no further use for them, they have taken away our country, and we have no further use for our buttons," showing a love of country which has been a Hawaiian trait up to the present time.

One of the sights in the streets of a Saturday afternoon in the olden times, which attracted a good deal of attention were two cavalcades. They were the returning from the afternoon ride of the King and the members of his court and the members of the Royal School.

The king's party mounted on spirited horses, the queen and the women usually dressed in bright colored silks or satins, with equally striking and varicolored riding *paus*, with hats trimmed with flowers and large wreaths of the sweet smelling maile, and often with their horses' necks decked with the same fragrant vine, occupied the whole width of the street from curb to curb.

They were all splendid riders, and strangers often gathered on the street as they swept gallantly by. Following them at some distance, came the young chiefs, the young ladies mounted on side saddles, in contrast to their elders, who rode the man's saddle. They too kept a well formed line as they swept by, and with these sights the day was brought to a close.

Those who remember having seen this display will probably be able to recall it with much more vivid distinctness, than I have here told it.

BERETANIA STREET

The boundaries of the old town may be said to have been, on the makai side, the waters of the harbor; on the mauka side, Beretania street; on the Waikiki side, the barren and dusty plain, and on the Ewa side, the Nuuanu stream.

There were few, if any, residences other than the straw houses of the natives mauka of Beretania street.

Beginning at the Ewa side of this latter street, we come first to the large Kaumakapili church on the mauka side. It was constructed of adobe bricks of large size, and the walls were some twelve or fifteen feet high; these were plastered without and within. The heavy timbers of the roof were from the mountains, and were covered with pili grass, forming probably one of the largest expanses of thatched roof there was in the town, if not upon the islands. It was a wonderful monument of the devotion and hard labor of the natives under the lead of their pastor, the Rev. Lowell Smith.

Kaumakapili Church (Paul Emmert, 1854)

The house of Mr. Smith was on the opposite side of the street and a little ways from the road. This was also of adobe, plastered, and was a home from which went out a large influence.

I can but bear a testimonial to the kindness of Mr. and Mrs. Smith to the stranger lad who had recently come to their shores, and for the hospitable home and welcome which they gave him in those early years.

It is a matter of much gratification that their influence still exists through children and grandchildren to the benefit of not only the Hawaiians, to whom the parents came especially to serve, but also to those who have come from beyond the sea.

Passing along in the direction of Waikiki, we come to the crossing of Nuuanu street. Not a building of any kind other than native houses on either side of the street.

On the makai side of the crossing of the two streets stood the residence of Dr. Rooke before alluded to.

Across the street mauka there was an adobe building, two stories high with a veranda, which after-wards became well known as the Commercial Hotel, of which the elder Macfarlane was manager.

The Commercial Hotel (Paul Emmert, 1854)

From here on to Fort street there was not a building other than those occupied by the natives. Fort street ended at Beretania street.

Continuing on our way, we come to a two-story house, built of coral, which was occupied by a Mr. Jones, a carpenter by trade, but at this time keeping a store.

Eli Jones House (Paul Emmert, 1854)

Still on our way, crossing a small lane, which ran makai, was the one-story, yet commodious, house of the Carter family. Captain and Mrs. J. O. Carter were known to all Honolulu by the kindliness of their manner, the warmth of their friendship, and enjoyed the respect and affection of the community in general.

They were both of them of fine figure and somewhat large proportions, and although Captain Carter was perhaps one of the heaviest-weight men in the town, he was one of the most graceful on the dancing floor there was in the place.

In later years, after the death of her husband, Mrs. Carter consented to use her home for the accommodation of visitors. No more hospitable dwelling was in the place; no more kindly reception given to the wayfarer, and it was a home indeed to many a traveler, and, especially to the captains of the ships which visited the port. Could they speak today they would respond with a most hearty aloha to the memory of the good and kind-hearted woman.

From here on the houses were but few and far between.

On the makai side of the road was the cottage occupied by Mr. and Mrs. William Paty, and beyond them the family of Mr. James Smith, an English gentleman, who, with his wife and family, had come up from the Society Islands and made their residence in Honolulu. In later years Mr. Smith was secretary of the celebrated Land Commission, and did most efficient and excellent service.

Across the street were the premises occupied by the English Consul, who arrived about this time – General Miller, a hero of the Chilean war of independence and a man of very marked individuality, strong feelings, and somewhat imperative in manner. He manifested the general characteristics of one who felt himself embodying the dignity and power of Great Britain.

General William Miller House (Paul Emmert, 1854)

Back of these premises the land sloped to Punchbowl Hill and this was the scene of a ludicrous incident.

Two of the men about town had come to have very strong feelings and prejudices against each other, which was somewhat generally known. Some of their acquaintances fostered this ill feeling, and finally induced one of the parties to send a challenge to the other to fight a duel.

The affair was supposed to be conducted with great secrecy; there were, however, the principals, the seconds, the doctor and a few privileged friends.

The combatants were placed in position, and at the word two pistols were discharged and there were two badly frightened men; but as the seconds had carefully provided that there should be no bullets in them the powder and wad could not inflict any serious injury.

The ludicrousness of the situation seemed to bring about good nature, and the town had a hearty laugh the next morning over the occurrence.

Later than the time of which I write, the Armstrong house was built, noticeable particularly from the fact that it was the first house built in Honolulu with chimney and fireplaces.

Rev. Richard Armstrong House, built 1846 (Paul Emmert, 1854)

From this house also have issued far-reaching influences which have told, and are still telling not only on the islands, but in the noble monumental institution, founded by Gen. Samuel C. Armstrong.

Washington Place was not built until later. Captain Dominis was away most of the time on his voyages, and his good wife superintended not only the building, noble and spacious as it was, but also the beautifying of the grounds with many tropical plants, which still adorn and make it the fit and beautiful home of the ex-Queen Liliuokalani.

Washington Place, completed 1847 (Paul Emmert, 1854)

We have thus described to the best of our recollection, after these sixty years and more, the streets as they were in those early days.

Kawaiahao Church

I will now close this long account of the old town with my recollections of the old Kawaiahao church. It was the old native framed thatched building.

If I remember rightly, some hundred and twenty feet long by some thirty or forty feet wide, the sides of thatch having been mostly eaten off by the stray horses, donkeys and cattle which had free access thereto. This was not without its conveniences, for instead of having only one door, of ingress and egress, it was very easy to pass between the upright posts into any part of the inside.

The floor was of earth, covered with lauhala mats. The settees were of native make. And were rude indeed. The pulpit was one of the old historical ones sent out from New England and did good service.

The preacher was the Rev. Richard Armstrong, father of our General Samuel C. Armstrong. He was a master of the idiomatic expressions of the Hawaiian language, and had acquired the intonations, inflections and gesticulations, the voice and manner of the people that he served so well.

With the history of the present church before your readers, I will not take the time and space to repeat it. May I say that it has some recollections that will forever associate it with those who, in former times, made it their resort.

In and out of its doors have gone the glad marriage procession, and in and out of the same doors has the music of the funeral dirge sounded up its aisles. Hail and farewell.

- The present church was first opened July 21, 1842-ED.

Kawaiahao Church (Paul Emmert, 1854)

In Conclusion

Recollections of the old streets bring back vividly those who used them; the merchants whose trade was of the conservative description, who did not know the word "hustle," the quiet even tenor of whose way was seldom disturbed by panics or failure. In the spring and fall whaling seasons, business was active "between seasons", Rip Van Winkle's sleep would not have been troubled.

The natives were in a large majority of those seen in the streets; the foreigners formed a small portion of the community, the Chinaman was a curiosity. The temporary influx of Jack on shore-liberty left a few dollars for horse hire. It was said that a native had trained a horse to allow Jack to ride out on the plains a way, then be unceremoniously landed on some sandy spot by the roadway when the horse would trot back to town and be hired out to another sailor to be served in the same manner.

The king and chiefs were not infrequently seen down town with a retinue of servants following. They were always dignified and courteous. When they bought it was generally by the quantity; the pay was not always prompt.

As I compare the old copper plate map of Honolulu engraved at Lahainaluna by some of the scholars, showing an almost bare plain with straw thatched houses here and there, a few cocoa nut trees growing scattered about, with scarce a frame house in the picture, and then turn to one of the recent panoramic photographs of King Brothers, showing a fine city with church spires, lofty buildings and stores that would do credit to the mainland.

I marvel at the change until I recall the thought that our revered and honored self-sacrificing' missionaries "builded better than they knew," and that in laying the foundations of religion, education, good government, others have built on what they began; progress and development have gone on apace and the islands will prove to be one of the most important outposts of our country.

> "Oft in the stilly night,
>
> * * * * * * *
>
> Fond memory brings the light
>
> Of other days around me."

Impressions of Honolulu, Past and Present
GORHAM D. GILMAN

Address at the Y.M.C.A hall on August 21, 1894, *The Hawaiian Star*, August 22, 1894

A small, but deeply interested audience listened to the address of Hon. Gorham D. Gilman, of Boston, at the Y.M.C.A. hall Tuesday evening. The speaker had selected as his topic, "Impressions of Honolulu, past and present." After an appropriate introduction by Mr. C.B. Ripley the distinguished gentleman said:

It gives me great pleasure to address you to-night because I am given an opportunity to review the past fifty years of my life. The subject I have chosen and upon which I will speak to you is "Impressions of Honolulu, past and present."

It was one afternoon in the month of May, 1841, when, after a voyage from Valparaiso on the ship Gloucester from Boston, we rounded Diamond Head. It was too late in the evening for us to make the port before dark so the order was given to reef topsails and stand off shore for the night. This was my first and last opportunity of acquiring the dignity to which most sailors aspire to – of passing the "weather earing," which I had the satisfaction of doing as a finishing touch to my sea-faring life.

The next morning early we were standing in for the anchorage. As we approached Diamond Head the trade winds were blowing fresh and free, a whale boat was descried approaching us and we "hove to" for the pilot, who proved in this case to be Mr. Stephen Reynolds, for many years a resident of Honolulu, and who occasionally performed the duties of a pilot.

It was a singular sight that greeted the eyes of our passengers, especially of the missionaries and their wives, of whom we had quite a large number on board. The apparently undistinguishable jargon of language, the earnest gesticulation and confused sounds of different cries as the boat was more or less in danger, in coming alongside of the ship, their half-clad forms washed by the spray that was breaking over them, were sights and sounds new and strange to all of us, and particularly so to feminine ears.

The mother of the President of the Republic was leaning over the side, and when she, with old mother Rice, saw these people they hastily retired to their cabins with the question arising in their minds, Are these the people with whom we have come to spend our lives? for in those days it was for a life service.

The ship was soon under way to the anchorage, which in due time we reached outside the bar, the wind being too strong for us to enter the harbor. It was not long before Governor Kekuanoa's double-banked barge, came alongside with some of the brethren of the Mission.

Arrangements were made for the party to land immediately, for the voyage had been a somewhat long one, and all were anxious once more to be on shore.

After all our missionary passengers had left, the captain with one or two passengers started in a boat we called the captain's gig, a fine-pulling cedar one for six oars. We were not long in coming up with the barge, and it was an almost head-to-head race between the six-oar boat and the eighteen-oar barge as to which would reach the wharf first. It was our good fortune to beat in this race, and I had the pleasure of throwing the bow-oar first onto the dock, finishing my twelve months' experience as a cabin boy and ordinary seaman.

The next morning I took up my position as clerk for the house of Ladd & Co., having made arrangements previously in Valparaiso with Mr. William Hooper one of the firm who was a passenger on board our ship.

As I remember, their store at that time stood at the foot of Nuuanu avenue, a small coral building situated at the head of the wharf which was but a landing place at that time. There were no stores or buildings on the makai side of what is now known as Queen street, from Paul Manini's to "Johnny Wright's shipyard" as it was familiarly called.

The appearance of the natives to us as newcomers was one of much novelty. Fashion had hardly as yet induced them to assume in very large quantities our style of clothing. The majority of men had not yet donned their pantaloons while the women were dressed mainly in what is now well known as the holoku. Their olive brown skins, their laughing eyes, pleasant faces and sweet voices, were a welcome to the strangers as comparatively few arrivals took place in those early days of as many passengers as our ship had brought. At the time everywhere was the word "aloha, aloha," as is the case today in the outer districts.

On the other islands where I have been I have found much of this sweet old originality. But associations have hardened their speech.

I remember one day away back in the forties I asked a native man to get a memorandum book for me. He straightway ordered his son to the task and at the same time ripped out a fearful oath. I was astonished and asked him what in the world he meant. He innocently replied that that was haole language and meant hurry up, quoting the sailors around the dock as his authority. This circumstance may have a wider application in illustrating the damaging effect of bad associations.

Between what is now Nuuanu avenue and Kaahumanu street, on the mauka side of Queen street, was what was then known as the fish market. It was an irregular collection of small booths of poles stuck in the ground, with cocoanut leaves for covering, and here and there native houses.

Mauka of this block, on what is now Merchant street, stood the store of Mr. Stephen Reynolds inclosed in a high wall built of blocks of coral. The building itself was of the same material. The one room of the store was reached by a flight of steps which showed years of wear.

The gentleman himself was a subject for a picture. Of somewhat short stature, light complexion, bald head with slight fringe of white hair, with an intelligent and speaking face he was an attractive person to meet. His dress usually consisted of a pair of nankeen trousers, white, unstarched bosom shirt, with one button at the throat, a large collar guiltless of confining necktie, with an occasional use of a loose nankeen jacket of the same color and material as the trousers, his head covered with a broad brim fine Panama hat without adornment of ribbon or other decoration.

He was one who would arrest attention from his striking appearance, and a man whose mental ability was above that of the average. He was occasionally engaged in some of the trials before the Courts of exciting cases and showed quite an acquaintance with the laws of the United States and other nations, and was, for an amateur, a very successful pleader.

I recall an order of a secret society, said to have been from the French, that was established in the upper rooms of the house of Mr. John Munn at the corner of Hotel and Fort streets, where it was said, the initiation was over a rough rugged road, with very scanty habilaments, from the depths of the cellar to the top of the lookout.

Just below this corner where now is Wichman's store, stood the store of one Mr. Webster who was quite small in stature, light in weight, but forcible in expression and fertile in wit. It was said that early one morning an English Admiral who had recently arrived in port was passing down the street and noticing this youthful appearing young man leaning against the door-post, looked up and saw the name of Webster. Addressing him he said, "Are you any relation to the great Daniel Webster"? "Yes," was the immediate reply, "I am his grandfather." The great contrast between the ponderosity of the great Daniel and the almost insignificant appearance of the young man gives a point to the story to those who knew the two that can scarcely be appreciated by a person of to-day.

One of the sights on a Saturday afternoon was the equestrians performance of almost all the people, especially the natives, who could possess themselves of a horse or mule to ride. The great feature of the afternoon, and its crowning act, was to see His Majesty the King with his retinue pass through the main street after their ride up the valley and out on the plain.

Coming to the northerly end of King street they were formed in two lines of some ten or twelve horsemen, with the King and the Queen in the centre and the highest chiefs flanked on either side, while behind them came those of lesser rank.

All the parties, dressed in their gayest riding apparel, the women with their long and vari-colored kaheis, and riding astride with jaunty hats and wreaths of flowers, and the sweet-scented maile, made quite an imposing appearance. They swept up the street at a full galop, having the right of way from curb to curb, and gaily passed on until the palace gates were reached and then the show of the afternoon was over.

Kamehameha III was a democratic King, a man among men, loving his people, being loved in return, always the same. Under him was started the first system of land tenure, and if the Hawaiian of to-day has parted with his land he has done so in the same way most others get rid of it.

Kamehameha III was a constitutional monarch and supported the constitution in accordance with his oath. He yearned for his people, and when he saw that they would be safer in the strong arms under the starry banner he did not hesitate to make the move in that direction.

King Kamehameha III was singularly unostentatious and personally exceedingly agreeable. Among his friends he treated them without reserve as companions, but they never forgot, no matter how intimate, the courtesy and consideration due his high rank. He was frequently seen about town, mounted on his favorite white horse and without guards, taking exercise.

I remember upon one occasion a stranger expressed a strong desire to see His Majesty. He happened to be passing at the time along the street on horseback, clad in his usual suite of white linen with Panama hat and without any decoration or guards or other special signs to indicate royalty. In reply to his wishes I said, "There he goes!" The eager question came back, "Where? Where?" I said, "There passing along on horseback." "Is that the King?" was his exclamation of astonishment. I said, "Yes." "Well, if I couldn't be more of a King than that I wouldn't be one."

There came a time when the Government seemed to be in a transition state or condition, and when it became necessary for some stronger power and mental capabilities to conduct the affairs of the nation.

Rev. Mr. Richards had been chosen years before as a guide and teacher to the King and royal chiefs and had well performed his duty. He was not, however an aggressive man; rather would he impart instruction in a courteous way and by his powers of persuasion endeavor to fix the truths, which he thought best to teach in the minds of his hearers.

Then there was Father Damon. Many a poor waif from society, drifted on these shores, was taken into Father Damon's double-seated open buggy and driven to his home. He cared not whether a man was a common sailor or an admiral, if he was in need he found Father Damon an angel, not in disguise, but opened and recognized by every one.

One thing may be said of our old friends the missionaries, that noble class of men who freely, willingly, resigned their ambitions, residence and business in their own land and came to these island with the sole purpose of devoting their lives in endeavoring to elevate those who had been so many years under the degradation of superstition, ignorance and selfish indulgence.

They came in those early days without any anticipations of returning to their native land; taking up their abode among the people and endeavoring to teach them by precept and practice that truth which afterwards came to be so well represented in the legend of the coat of arms of the country, that "The life of the land is established in righteousness."

Many a traveler over the islands in the forties and early fifties was feign to accept the open hospitality of the mission families, where the stranger, so be that he bore the garb and manner of a gentleman, was free to come, remain and go when he pleased.

In the early days, while the men in pursuit of business, pleasure or excitement would come to reside upon the Island, Honolulu for long years could boast of but very few ladies in what would be called "foreign society."

It is the matter within memory, when at the house of Mr. and Mrs. William Paty of Beretania street, who were entertaining a company of friends, there were found a sufficient number of ladies to form a double quadrille, the first that was danced in the city.

On the same evening a letter was shown which had arrived that day from Mazalan, Mexico, which was in answer to one which had been sent from Honolulu five months before. It was noticeable from the short space of time it then took to send and receive a letter from the United States.

The business community was thrown into quite a state of excitement at one time by the announcement that "Cheap John" had opened a store on the corner of Nuuanu and Hotel street, where he was offering cotton cloth at six yards for $1. This was a revelation and a revolution.

Formerly the prices had been, for what would be termed a nicer quality of goods, like turkey-red cotton, two yards for $1. Fair calicos were sold three yards for $1, and scarcely any such material was sold better than four yards for $1; and when these young men from Australia opened their store and broke prices there was consternation among the old regulars. Meetings were held and plans laid for suppressing such unheard-of innovation.

The changes that have come over everything since those olden days is very marked. The grass hut has about disappeared and has been replaced by board dwellings from Columbia river. This illustrates the progress and I am glad to see it.

I deplore the diminution in numbers of the Hawaiian race. When I reached here in 1841 there were 130,000, and now there are less than 40,000. But the question which lies closest to my heart is, what is the future of the Hawaiian people.

I have seen around me signs of wonderful material property. Never has there been so much land under cultivation, never so much intelligence apparent upon the thoroughfares, never such prosperity as seen at every hand. The future must be based upon stable government. Build upon the foundation of justice, right and truth.

Though an American, with all of my interests in the United States, I love Hawaii nei next to, it not equal with, my own land. And the sweetest word my mother taught me to lisp, a word I say to you at parting, is – Aloha!

A Half Century Gone
GORHAM D. GILMAN

The Hawaiian Star, August 23, 1894

In Mr. Gilman's address at the Y.M.C.A. hall Tuesday evening upon the subject "Impressions of Honolulu Past & Present," the speaker dwelt a great deal upon the city as it was fifty years ago. Since then the gentleman has furnished the STAR with a paper entitled "Reminiscences of Honolulu Fifty Years Ago," which will be published in installments in this paper from day to day. Taking up the subject from the description of Ladd & Co's. store in the address the paper says:

On the opposite side of Nuuanu street was the store of one who was familiarly called "old Uncle Grimes." He was also a man who had been many years upon the island had conducted quite a successful miscellaneous trade with the natives and was in comfortable circumstances, although not of so decided personal characteristics as was Mr. Reynolds. It was in his store that a word was coined which became of national usage. He had in his employ a somewhat elderly good-natured native, who was in some way connected by marriage with Mr. Grimes, and was a privileged character in the store, and occasionally acted as a salesman. When the natives came in to purchase calico or dress good, particularly the women, they would say to Maumanuahi, which was his name, "1 Maumanuahi", trying to induce him to give a larger measure. This extra length, or extra gift, which he was persuaded to grant, became the custom among the people to ask of the other store keepers generally, and was commonly used by the natives when asking for larger portion of anything that they were buying than a strict measure would be.

Continuing mauka, on the northerly side of Nuuanu street, we come to the premises of the Hudson Bay Co.'s Agent, enclosed in a high plastered stone wall with strong gates. Within were the offices of George Pelly, Esq., the companies' representative. There English customs and English observances were largely used.

Still mauka on the corner of King street was the Blonde hotel where the rubicund face and form of him who was familiarly termed "Joe Booth" kept a hostelry, more for the gratification of the bibulous than those who were hungry for food. He kept this place for many years and was a well-known citizen, good natured and kindly, and exceedingly patriotic in his attachment to his mother country.

Turning to the left we come to the residence of one Isaac Montgomery who had built one of the first of the two-story business places on the street. He also was a British subject and a man of somewhat peculiar temperament, at times, being somewhat noted for a free use of his individual liberty. Still he was one with many good qualities.

Across the street were the premises of Captain John Meek, an old resident from the United States, who was the father of quite a family. He was a large sized man, had acquired considerable real estate or landed property and was the owner of large herds of cattle. He was one of the three persons who acted as pilots, old Captain Adams being the third.

The latter had a place a mile or two out to the north where he was always ready and willing to receive his friends. He also had a place farther to the south of Hotel street. It was in his premises that the first lodge room of the order of Odd Fellows was instituted where a few friends who had accidently met at Honolulu were of a sufficient number to constitute opening officers. I believe I am the only living member of those who were first initiated in that queer and quaint lodge room.

At this time there was but one store on Merchant street between Nuuanu and King [Fort – ED]. It was owned and kept by the Messrs. Paty Brothers. Captain John Paty (later styled Commodore after making one hundred passages) of the trio of brothers was the commander of a packet that used to make its regular trips as the season would admit, to and from the Coast.

Mr. Thomas Cummings had a small store on the mauka corner of Fort and Merchant streets. He also was an old-time resident. An agreeable and gentle gentleman, though very quiet, he had many friends, both of his own nationality (which was English) and among the American residents. His son has since been honored in the Cabinets of the Government.

Among other business men at this time was Mr. William Ladd, the head of the house of Ladd & Co., which consisted of Messrs. Ladd, Brinsmade and Hooper. Mr. Ladd's erect form, methodical manner and precise ways marked him as a man of business. A man of few words but large ideas, which were not always successful in their being carried out. It was this firm, under the superintendence of Mr. Hooper, who owned the first sugar plantation on the island of Kauai.

At that time there were but few or no cattle broken to the yoke. It is said that the first plowing was done under Mr. Hooper's direction by a gang of some forty men, who drew the plough in lieu of oxen, there being none of the latter to be had, and it was in this rude way the ground was first broken for the planting of the sugar cane. From this small beginning what a great industry has sprung up!

Mr. Brinsmade was the American Consul, a gentleman who had formerly been a clergyman in the United States. A man of impulsive, warm-hearted nature, who made friends everywhere and whose pleasing manners made him an agreeable companion.

This firm was known generally as the "missionary firm," two or three members of it belonging to the orthodox church, and it had some special understanding and arrangement with the members of the American Mission in regard to purchase of goods.

The other store keepers were not known generally as having very much interest in spiritual matters of the theological kind, whatever their interests may have been in spirits of a different quality.

Among the most respected merchants of the place and deservedly popular was Mr. Charles Brewer, who for many years conducted a most honorable business career and had troops of friends among the natives and foreigners with whom he came in contact.

A little anecdote is told of his good nature at the expense of one of his missionary brethren, who had called on morning from a sense of duty to see him. He found Mr. Brewer very busily engaged in unpacking a very large cask of hardware containing an almost innumerable number of little papers of tacks, brads, screws, etc., etc.

Mr. Brewer in his white linen suit without coat or collar was busily engaged in diving to the depths of this capacious cask and hunting out its contents, when after a little pause, he was addressed by the good brother without much preliminary introduction. "Mr. Brewer have you any interest in the Kingdom of Heaven?" It was certainly a somewhat singular question, unlooked for under the peculiar circumstances, but with a genial smile which was a characteristic of the large hearted man, he replied, "I have a good deal more interest in this cask of hardware just now."

The good brother having discharged his sense of duty, retired feeling, that he had had a pleasant answer to his question if not as satisfactory as he could have wished.

Among the best of men who were styled mechanics that had arrived, and for many years did arrive to make their business in Honolulu were two young men of excellent character and reputation, and what too often was not the case were masters of their profession as cabinet makers. Messrs. R.A.S. Wood and Wm. C. Parke were known from the excellent quality of their work and their stability of character, particularly the latter, which for many years made him so worthily popular in Honolulu.

It used to be said that a native would be willing to die if he could have the promise of being buried in one of the handsome Koa coffins which were turned out from this establishment.

The latter gentleman of the firm builded better than he knew, for while undoubtedly some of his good mechanical work can still be found yet the character for integrity and uprightness which he showed among the people for a residence of forty years is the best eulogy of the man.

Honolulu harbor at the time of which I write had not reached its popularity of later years, but there were occasionally ships of war and commonly a good number of whalers made this their port for supplies.

Among the earlier residents was Mr, Robert L. Davis, who was born on the Islands and educated in the United States and was of a quiet and refined nature, he enjoyed a joke with as cool a manner and unmoved face as any man in the community. It was quite a favorite amusement of his to engage some returning whaling skipper in conversation and draw out form him the story of his voyage, while he enlivened his companion with a narrative of most wonderful exploits of the whaling killing line in which he made himself the hero and which were entirely drawn from his imagination and the good memory with which he had retained all the wondrous stories which he had heard.

Excerpt from Infancy of Honolulu
GORHAM D. GILMAN

The Hawaiian Star, August 27, 1894

It was in the early fifties that the first steamer to ply between the islands arrived from San Francisco. She was formerly a Boston harbor boat called "The Wheeler." The natives expressed their wonder at this new style of craft by calling her the akamae (skillful), referring to the peculiar construction and use of steam as a propelling power. Her frail and peculiar side wheel build made her ill fitted to contend with the strong trade winds that blew in the channels between the islands, and many stories of hair-breadth escapes could be told of her trips.

Steamer Akamai (Paul Emmert, 1854)

One in particular may be worth noting, as she had on board as passengers at that time Chief Justice Lee and the Minister of Education and Interior, Mr. Armstrong, with the usual number of natives and some other passengers of less note.

Leaving the anchorage at Lahaina she was found to be heavily laden with a cargo of sugar. On her passage to Honolulu she encountered a very severe southerly gale of wind. She was the entire day in making this passage, which is usually made in a few hours. As night drew on the situation became critical. The order was passed by the officer to the men that it was either pump or sink.

As we drew near the entrance to the harbor we could see a stranded ship that had been forced by the gale upon the reef. Darkness soon shut out all hop of being able to clearly discern the entrance. The waves were breaking with great force along the reef, almost hiding the narrow passage to the channel.

A council was held as to whether the steamer should be turned head to sea and an attempt made to ride out the gale or whether an effort should be made to reach the land.

Fortunately an old and experience pilot was on board, who took the helm from one who refused to be further responsible for the guidance of the boat in the darkness.

At this juncture a stronger blast of wind than usual swept over the boat and the harbor, and lifted the heavy cloud veil so that the outline of the valley could be discovered beyond.

The practiced eye of the old pilot saw this opportunity and turning the wheel quickly, headed the steamer towards the entrance and we were soon riding upon the crest of the waves that were bearing us upon the shore, whether to strike upon the reef or glide into the still water was for a few moments a most anxious question.

Fortunately for us and for the country's sake, in the persons of the illustrious officers of the government that were with us, a good Providence seemed to guide our way and with a few tremendous surges of the waves curving around us we were slid into the still water of the harbor.

As our escape became evident, hand grasped hand, and unbidden tears rolled down the cheeks, while voices were silent, incapable of speech, but unuttered prayers were send heavenward in thanks for our deliverance.

A few moment later, friends who had been anxiously watching for the boat, having heard our signals of distress from beyond the reef, were surrounding us and ere long we were enjoying the hospitality of warmhearted friends in the quiet and pleasant homes beyond the reach of the storm.

Gorham D. Gilman

GORHAM D. GILMAN.

Born in Hallowell, Maine, in 1822, Gorham Dummer Gilman went to sea in 1840 at age 18, eventually ended up in Hawaii via Valparaiso 'round the Horn in May 1841.

He took a job as the youngest clerk at the store of Ladd & Co., founded in 1833 by Peter Brinsmade and William Ladd, also from Hallowell, Maine. They were known as the "pious traders" due to Brinsmade attending Yale Theological Seminary from 1828 to 1829.

Ladd & Co. built a large stone warehouse on the waterfront and initially used the hulk of a sunken ship for a wharf. In 1835, they owned the first large-scale commercial sugar plantation at Koloa.

Peter Brinsmade was appointed American consular agent in 1839 and was promoted to Consul in 1844. With the consular office in the same building, Gilman often worked there too.

By 1846 Gilman had his own store, selling goods from sailing ships. He learned Hawaiian and was known as Kilimana.

```
            GOODS RECEIVED
   PER SHIP CHARLES and for sale at the
       store occupied by G. D. GILMAN:
   Asst'd Prints, Gingham, printed Cashmere,
   Figured and white check Muslin,
   Madras, red and blue Handkerchiefs,
   Spool Cotton, blue and white cotton Thread,
   Tape, colored Cambric, linen Towels,
   Brown and bleached linen Drill,
   Damask and worsted Table Covers,
   Linen Diaper, assorted Hoisery, wool Frocks,
   Indigo and mazarine blue Cottons,
   Satin Jeans, kremlin Stripes, brown Cottons,
   Blue Drill, Flannel, &c., &c.
                  —ALSO—
     Sheet Lead, loaf Sugar, Cigars, Soap, Candles,
   jars Prunes, handled Axes, &c.
     A few of Paty's best Perfumes and cold Cream.
     s 19                                      tf
```

Like many others, Gilman left Hawaii for the California gold rush, but returned in the spring of 1849.

```
G. D. GILMAN.
KALEPOLEPO, MAUI.
Feb. 1851.                              H. I.
☞ Potatoes furnished to order.         1y-41
```

By 1851 he had a store in Maui, and in May of 1851 he partnered with Benjamin F. Bolles who had a large ship chandlery business in Honolulu.

In March of 1852 he had his own ship's supply and general merchandise store in Lahaina

```
G. D. GILMAN,
SHIP CHANDLERY
AND
GENERAL MERCHANDIZE.
LAHAINA, MARCH 15, 1852-tf-45
```

In October 1853 Gilman teamed up with Captain F.C. Smith of the ship *Eliza Adams*.

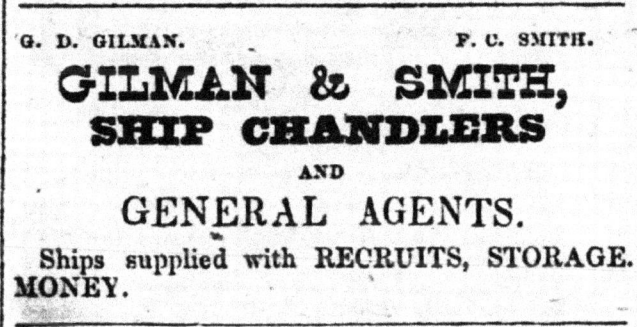

Gilman was also briefly an auctioneer in Lahaina in early 1854.

G. D. GILMAN,
AUCTIONEER,
LAHAINA, MAUI,
Feb. 18, 1854.-1yr-41   Hawaiian Islands.

The partnership with Capt. Smith was dissolved on July 3, 1854, and Gilman continued as Gilman & Co. in Lahaina.

Due in part to the demise of the whaling fleet, he put his business up for sale in January 1860.

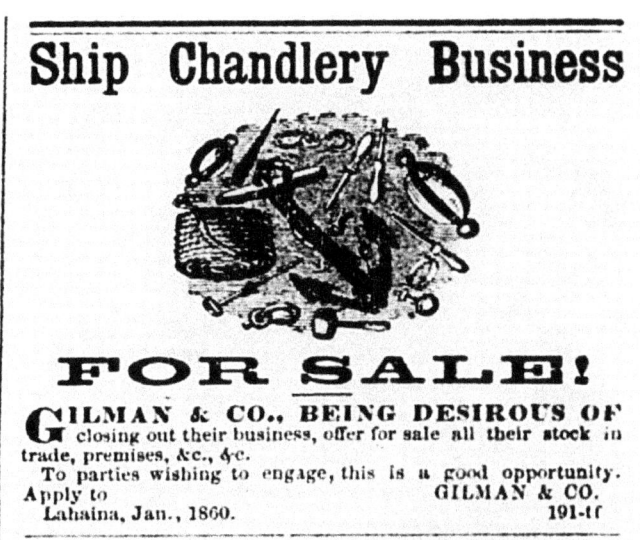

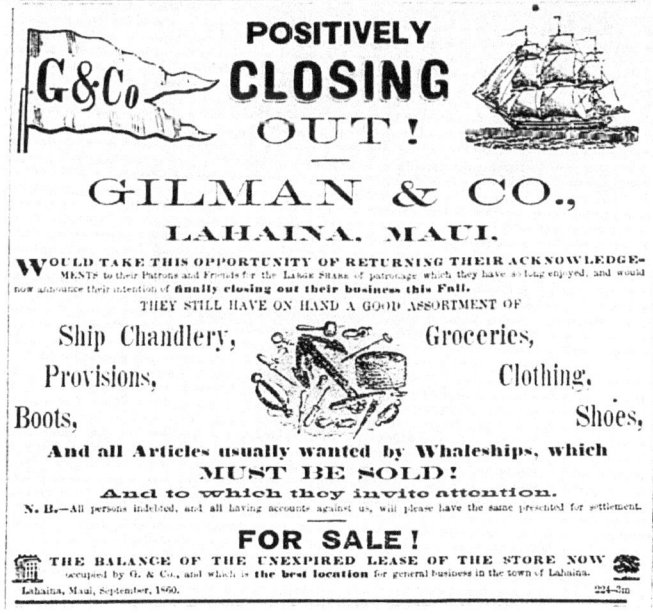

He closed Gilman & Co. on November 21, 1860, and returned to Boston to join his brothers in the Gilman Brothers wholesale and patent medicine drug business.

In July 1866, Gilman was one of the founding members of the Hawaiian Club of Boston along with James Hunnewell, Captain Charles Brewer, General Marshall, E.P. Bond, Benjamin Pitman, R.W. Wood, Warren Goodale, David M. Weston – all former residents of Hawaii "who still and always will retain an *aloha* for the land of their adoption".

> Mr. G. D. Gilman, a former resident of the Islands, who gave a princely reception to Queen Kapiolani and party at his house in Boston, has been invested by the King with the insignia of Knight Commander of the Royal Order of Kalakaua.

The Hawaiian Gazette, October 9, 1888

> The friends of Mr. G. D. Gilman, who formerly resided here and is now a resident of Newton, near Boston, Mass., will be glad to hear of his election to the "General Court" or Legislature of Massachusetts. He was chosen by a majority of 1,500 over his Democratic rival. Mr. Gilman is a man of large experience and liberal views, and his Republican constituency have done a wise thing to select him to represent them in their provincial assembly.

The Honolulu Advertiser, December 1, 1888

Gilman returned to visit Hawaii in 1894 at age 72, staying several months. In addition to visiting friends and traveling, he preached a sermon at Kawaiahao Church and gave a lecture at the YMCA on August 21, 1894.

Appointed the Hawaiian Consul in Boston in 1893, Gilman wrote many articles about Hawaii, and gave "four hundred volumes on Hawaii" to the Oahu College Library. He died October 3, 1909.

"Hawaii has no firmer friend abroad than Mr. G"

APPENDIX

Reminiscences of John Cook, Kamaaina and Forty-Niner

Published by New Freedom Press in 1927, these recollections of John Cook, English-born carpenter and builder who lived in Hawaii from 1844 to 1916, were written in 1909 when he was 85 years old.

Reminiscences

OF

John Cook

KAMAAINA

and

Forty-Niner

Honolulu
1927

NOTE.—John Cook, some of whose random recollections are given here, was born in England in 1823. He arrived at Maui in 1844, and after a residence in the Hawaiian Islands of 72 years, died on Maui in 1916. These reminiscences were written in 1909, seven years before Mr. Cook died.

Reminiscences

I was born in 1823. My father was a carpenter in the Royal Navy. The type of men-o'-war ships in which he had served were much the same as those of Nelson's time; they were still in reality "the wooden walls of old England," and had not yet been replaced by ugly monsters of steel, driven by steam and filled chock a-block with a mass of machinery. After leaving the sea service, which was chiefly spent on the North Atlantic station, my father became head carpenter in Deptford Dockyard, finally retiring on an allowance to the west of England, whence he originally hailed. I was born and brought up in the little old world Dorsetshire village of Charmouth, situated on the sea coast about halfway between Lyme Regis and Bridport. All along the coast of Dorset are a number of fine cliffs and headlands covered with short turf, on which are bred the celebrated Southdown sheep. Those who wish to know more about Dorsetshire ought to peruse Sir Frederick Treves' book, which I read recently. This book tells all about my old homeland, with its cool cider, its miles of hawthorn hedges covered with sweet smelling May blossoms, and its quaint old towns and villages. Dorsetshire is the Wessexshire of Thomas Hardy the novelist, who is himself a native of the shire. The life of the people is well described in some of his novels. Dorsetshire is best known as being the home of many celebrated sailors. It has furnished thousands of seamen to the Royal Navy and the Mercantile Marine from Queen Elizabeth's time down to the present day.

Well, to return to myself. Having learnt my trade as a carpenter in my native village, I joined the Royal Navy, but my stay there did not last very long. One day, shortly after joining, I was sent ashore as one of a boat party, under charge of a young cub of a midshipman. Whilst waiting on the beach, the midshipmite gave me an order to do something, accompanied by rather violent adjectives, and in return I knocked him down and then skipped out. I managed to escape by smuggling aboard a trading sloop bound for Fowey in Cornwall. After this I made several voyages abroad and in 184— shipped on a troopship bound for New Zealand. Afterwards I engaged as a carpenter at Sydney, N.S.W., on board the American ship Lewis of New Bedford, Captain Tollman, bound for a whaling cruise to the north. After returning from our cruise, we anchored in Lahaina roadstead on 16th September, 1844, and on the following day I first set my foot on the Hawaiian, or as it was then known, the Sandwich Islands. Captain Tollman, by the bye, in later years returned to the islands in command of the "Midas," and died and was buried at Hilo where I have seen his grave.

LAHAINA IN THE FORTIES

In the forties, the whaling industry was in full swing, and on the day we arrived at Lahaina, there must have been between 40 and 50 whalers anchored in the channel. In 1845, the year after I arrived, 500 whaleships touched at Lahaina. In these days, the landing for boats at Lahaina was at the canal, and boats pulled right in. Nowadays the entrance to the canal has been allowed to get chocked up with sand and mud. The present wharf did not exist then. The canal was at the south side of the fort, which stood on the ground where the present court house is erected. Lahaina was then, as at the present time, made up of one long street along the beach, with a number of native huts among the cocoanut and breadfruit trees—the celebrated "Ulumalu." Nearly all the houses were constructed of grass, with thatch roofs, and there were also a few adobe houses scattered along the water front.

I wasn't an hour ashore before I struck a job as a carpenter with John Halstead or Johnnie Liilii as he was called. Johnnie Liilii afterwards left Lahaina to establish a business at Kalepolepo, further along the coast, and which was then the shipping point for produce brought down from the Kula district.* Norton and Kip succeeded to Halstead's business and I continued to work for them. Kip eventually went to Los Angeles and became a Mormon, and Norton, known as Jack, but whose real name was Giles Norton, died a few years ago at Molokai.

The work hours for mechanics in those days were from sunrise to sunset, and the usual wages were $2 per day, paid in Chilean, Mexican, Peruvian or Bolivian silver dollars, half-dollars, quarters or reals (hapa walu) and sometimes a gold Peruvian doubloon worth $16.

The fort, long since knocked down, served as the Governor's residence and the gaol. By the time I reached these islands, the sandal wood trade was pau, and the kukui oil business was dying out. Lahainaluna school had been started about four years before

---

*Johnnie Liilii's house at Kalepolepo, built of koa, is still standing, and occupied by his grand-daughter, Mrs. Charles Wilcox.

my arrival, and I have several times, in 1844-5, done jobbing work up there. It was a straggling place and was then under the charge of the Rev. Mr. Alexander, father of Professor W. D. Alexander. He was a fine old man.

Board and lodging for white men could be got for $3 per week. I boarded with Mr. and Mrs. Hugh McIntyre, who kept a sailors' and mechanics' boarding house on the beach. Hugh McIntyre was the father of Hugh McIntyre, who kept a grocery store at the corner of Fort and King streets, and who afterwards joined with Henry May & Co. and Waterhouse & Co. Another child of old Hugh was Mrs. John S. Walker, Sr., and many's the time I dandled her in my arms when she was a baby. Old Hugh McIntyre was a ship's carpenter. Had learnt his trade at Greenock, Scotland, and had come out to these islands via Tahiti. Young Hugh was brought up when a child at Tahiti by his maternal uncle, George Greig, afterwards interested in Fanning's Island. Young Hugh was brought up to the islands to rejoin his father and mother by this uncle. At the time when the gold fever broke out, in 1848-9, old Hugh sailed with his family for California. He kept an eating house in San Francisco and made some money. Subsequently he returned to Honolulu and started a grocery and bakery on the corner of Fort and King streets, where the First National Bank now stands. George Greig for a while was clerk in his store.

Another oldtimer who used to live at Lahaina in the forties was Henry Curtis, an Englishman and a carpenter by trade. When the gold excitement started Curtis was anxious to leave for California, but as he was married to a native woman, he had first of all to find a bondsman to become security for his return within six months. I went upon his bond. However, he did not go at that time, but did so later on. I also became bondsman for Giles Norton, one of my employers, who also tried his luck at the gold fields.

By the time that I arrived at the islands most of the old race of Kamehameha's warriors had died and there were very few of the higher chiefs left. The late King Kalakaua was then a boy of 12 years of age. His sister, Makaeha, later known as Queen Liliuokalani, was then a young kid of 6 years or so, but neither of these two were considered of any importance in these days. Kauikeaouli (Kamehameha III.) was then 31 years old, and but the year previous had his sovereignty restored to him by Admiral Thomas. Our old friend, the motto "Ua mau ke ea o ka aina," which now-a-days is to be seen engraved on all fancy brooches, coins, etc., was but recently born. Alexander Liholiho, afterwards Kamehameha IV., was a boy of 12 years, and Lot, who succeeded him as Kamehameha V., was 14.

I've seen as many as 1,000 sailors ashore at Lahaina at one time, and it may well be believed that the place was anything but "The Paradise of the Pacific." It was then more correctly termed "The Brothel of the Pacific." In the season when the whaling fleet returned from the north to recruit, I have seen schooner after schooner arriving from Hawaii, packed full with women—young and middle-aged—who had come, either on their own account, or who had been brought by their parents, in order to make money by selling themselves to the sailors. The same thing happened at Honolulu, where the women would flock from Kauai for the same purpose. Later on, when living at Kauai, I several times tried to dissuade women from getting aboard the island schooners, and pointed out to them the sad results which would follow. Many's the time one would see a fine healthy, strapping young girl, with fresh, clear complexion, leave Kauai and return in six months or so with her face all blotched and sodden, an utter physical wreck, who would help to further spread disease like wildfire through the countryside. It is true the Hawaiians had not much self restraint, yet they certainly did not get any good lessons from the majority of white men who visited the islands in the early days; rather they were induced to make utter beasts of themselves. Nowadays, very few specimens survive of the old pure-bred Hawaiian race of six-foot warriors and stately dames. Nothing is left but a remnant of mixed blood.

Outside Lahaina, I did not explore Maui very much. The furthest I traveled was once as far as Kahului in the company of Isaac Adams and several others. Kahului consisted then of a few fishing huts on the beach, and no one would then have dreamt of its having a breakwater, a bank or having in its vicinity one of the largest sugar plantations in the world. The ride to and from Lahaina was a rough one, and as I had hitherto been more at home on the deck of a vessel than astride a saddle, I felt rather sore for several days after my return.

Jim Young, an illegitimate son of old John Young, the companion of Kamehameha I., was then Governor of Maui. Jim was therefore a half brother of John Young II. (Keoni Ana). Jim Young was one of the retainers who formed part of the train of Liholiho and Kamamalu when they visited England in 1824. One

7

day when Jim was in London, he left the hotel in the Adelphi where Liholiho and suite resided and went off for a stroll by himself down the Strand. He noticed, stuck up at the entrance door of a bootmaker's shop, a miniature gilded shoe, which served as a sort of sign board. Jim knew the value of gold and this big lump of what appeared to him to be made of the precious metal, was too much for his cupidity. He tore the gold shoe from its bracket, and bolted down the street with his prize. He was noticed, pursued and captured by a policeman and brought before a magistrate. It was found, however, that Jim could speak but a few words of English, and on enquiries being made they discovered who Jim was and returned him to his hotel. I have listened to Jim telling his adventures and what he had seen in London. He was a great "Pelekane" man.

I have played billiards several times at Lahaina with Kamehameha III. The common natives (men) went around clothed in the malo or breech clout, and without hat or shoes, but some of the higher class were better clad. I soon picked up a knowledge of the native lingo and can now converse quite fluently, although perhaps not quite grammatically. In later years, when living on Kauai, I've been for six months at a stretch without hearing a word of English spoken. The natives of Kauai when speaking used the "T" sound in place of "K." So far back as I can remember, the "R" sound had disappeared and "L" had taken its place.

About the time I was at Lahaina, there had been experiments tried on a small scale in growing sugar cane between Lahaina and Kaanapali, but they did not pay and were given up. Jim Nowlein, or as he was usually known, Gipsy Jim, grew some sugar cane up in the Makawao district and made molasses out of it for sale. Gipsy Jim was the father of Sam Nowlein. He was a "Sydney duck." He lived in a house opposite to the fort, where the court house now stands, and until quite recently the walls of his house were still there. I think the land where Gipsy Jim's house is, or was, was bought by the late Mrs. Campbell Parker (herself a native of Lahaina) and deeded to the public to serve as a small park. Another old resident of Lahaina when I was there was Peter Treadway. I was present at his marriage to Sally Nowlein, a daughter of Gipsy Jim.

8

OLD TIMERS AT LAHAINA

Some other names of persons that I recall as living in Lahaina when I was there, are George White, Charles Cockett, H. A. Peirce, then a clerk for Brewer & Co., Thomas Phillips, who was a sort of rancher; E. Saffery, who kept a beer house at Lahaina and whose half-white descendants are here. Then there were Doctors Tennant and Hawke, both ex-whale ship surgeons. At that time all English whaleships carried surgeons.

At a big luau given at the cocoanut grove, Lahaina, Kamehameha III. presided over the feast and shook hands with all the foreigners present. After the spread was finished, Dr. Hawke (Hawkes?) got down on his knees in front of the king and begged his majesty to give him the house and lot where he lived. The king was disgusted with his conduct and said, "Hoopailua ka haole." Dr. Peabody was also stationed at Lahaina. He was drowned on the passage to Honolulu. Queen Emma adopted his daughter, Lucy, who is still living. Two other names that I remember are Charlie Copp, tailor and father of the present magistrate of Makawao. Tom Hennessy, keeper of a bowling alley, lived at Lahaina. He came to the islands about 1838 and died about three years ago.

KOA TIMBER

Koa was principally used for building purposes. Partitions, floorings, ceilings, etc., all were of koa lumber. A small supply of rough Nor West was to be had from the Columbia river, brought to the islands in whaleships. The first cargo of redwood arrived in the "Sabine," which brought the news of the California gold discovery. Koa used to cost from one and one-half to three cents per foot. Jim Fay and Macy and Louzada used to bring quite of lot of koa from the Kohala mountains, where it was cut into planks by whip saws. The koa that comes from the mountains is harder and will last longer, and is not so liable to be attacked by the koa worms. Quite a large number of men used to gain a livelihood by sawing koa lumber on the slopes of Mauna Kea and Mauna Loa. They would vary their life by hunting wild cattle for their hides. George Hardy, who died some years ago at Honokaa, when he first came to this country, followed the free life on the slope of Maunakea. George Hardy, by the way, was an old navy carpenter, and had served as such in both the British and American navies before coming to settle on the islands.

9

DISCOVERY OF GOLD IN CALIFORNIA

I worked in Lahaina until 1848, when the news of the discovery of gold in California reached the islands. I would have left for the coast as soon as the news came, but I happened to be laid up with rheumatism. Times in the off season became dull in Lahaina, and I took passage for Honolulu on the first three-masted schooner ever built in the islands. She was built for Jack Shaw or Jack Straw, restaurant keeper at Lahaina, close to where Nowlein's house was, and I helped to build her. I forget her name, in fact, I don't think she was then christened, as she was on her first trip and had to come to Honolulu to get her license.

HONOLULU IN THE FORTIES

My first lodgings in Honolulu in 1848 was in a two-roomed grass cottage situated on Alakea street, where the Young garage now is, below the Wicke premises. There was a big algaroba tree in front of the house. A bench was at the foot of the tree, and I and other young fellows used to sit under the shade in the evening and sing songs and play on the fiddle and clarionet. The statement printed on the board nailed on to the front of the algaroba tree in the Roman Catholic yard on Fort street to the effect that such tree was the first algaroba tree planted in the Hawaiian islands, is scarcely correct. When I came to Honolulu in 1848, on the spot where the R. C. Cathedral tree now grows, there stood a shed in which Vida, Chilean consul, stabled a fine black stallion, which he sold to Charlie Vincent, the builder, who, on his part, afterwards resold to Kamehameha III. for $1,000. When I came here there was not only the full-grown algaroba tree on Alakea street which I speak of, but there was another which stood near the corner of Merchant and Fort streets on the spot where the warehouse to the rear of the Pacific Hardware Company's store now is. There was another algaroba tree in the vicinity of the English cathedral grounds, but I cannot recall the exact site of this one. On Kauai also, at Koloa, when I went in 1850, there was an old algaroba tree growing at the Charles Tobey plantation. The Tobey plantation was one of the earliest sugar cane plantations, and was afterwards bought by Reynolds and Gilmore, and later on, I suppose, was incorporated with the Koloa plantation.

10

I stayed in Honolulu from New Year's Day, 1848, to May, 1849, when I sailed for San Francisco to try my luck at the mines. Arrived in San Francisco July, 1849. Did not make my pile in California. Was in San Francisco during the exciting days of the Vigilantes.

From California I went up to Oregon and came back as mate of a vessel to San Francisco. Left San Francisco in December, 1849, and arrived back at Honolulu in January, 1850.

.At the present time (September, 1909) there are few white foreign born residents who have lived in the Hawaiian islands for a longer period than I have. Two there are that I recall at this moment, viz., Mr. Bailey of Maui and Mrs. Rice of Lihue. There are a few white Hawaiian-born residents who were born some years previous to my arrival here, but they were then but children, whereas I was a young man of 21 when I landed on the islands.

Francisco de Paulo Marin, or Manini. I remember old Paul very well, but do not remember having spoken to him. He had three sons—Paul, Frank and John, and one daughter—with all of whom I was acquainted. Manini homestead lay between Maunakea and Nuuanu streets. Probably the lane called Marine street was called after him.

Doctor Rooke was a thin, short man. Married Fanny Young, a sister of John Young II., premier at the time. Fanny Young was a daughter of John Young I. Dr. Rooke built the house now known as Queen Emma house on the southeast corner of Nuuanu and Beretania streets. It was built before I came to Honolulu. The house is now entirely neglected and used by Japanese as a warehouse for old bottles, bags and junk, and the former garden as a storage place for stone ballast, firewood, etc. It's a wonder that the heirs of Dr. Rooke do not fix up the house or else knock it down altogether. To allow it to remain in its present state is a disgrace to the memory of Queen Emma. Dr. Rooke, when I first knew him, carried on a consulting practice. He was not in the habit of visiting his patients. He was an old ship's doctor previous to settling on the islands. Dr. Rooke was a fine, jovial man who loved a joke, but at the same time was a good business man.

Robert Boyd kept the old Blonde hotel, which was situated in Bethel street where Castle & Cooke's brick warehouse now is. I believe it is now occupied as a storehouse by E. O. Hall

& Son. I met Bob at the "Shades," a gambling house in San Francisco in '49, where he was a billiard marker.

John Kellett was an old English sailor, father of Danson Kellett, who worked for such a long time with T. H. Davies & Co. John Kellett owned part of the land where Davies & Co.'s premises are on Kaahumanu street, or Queen street, and sold same, I think, to Henry Skinner. John Kellett afterwards settled at Hanalei, Kauai. His daughter, Betsy, married a Captain Hadfield, and another to Friedenberg.

William French was a small-sized man. Lived on Alakea street where the entrance to the Hawaiian Hotel is. The first windmill in Honolulu was erected in his yard in the middle of what is now Alakea street and opposite to where the Pacific Club is. His only child married Bush, who kept a grocery store where the Oddfellows' building on Fort street is. Mrs. Bush lived on Emma street.

Alexander Cartwright and Bruce Cartwright were two brothers who kept a grocery store. Alexander Cartwright was the father of Bruce Cartwright (who also has a son named Bruce) and Alexander Cartwright for some years past living in California, I believe.

Savidge and May were the first to start a grocery store of any size worth speaking of. Opened on King street between the Hoffschlaeger building and the saloon at the corner. Savidge was head of the firm. Henry May went on a visit to England, and during his absence, Savidge managed to get the firm heavily involved. May returned and took charge, Savidge being reduced to the position of bookkeeper. Savidge was married to May's sister. The business was afterwards carried on by Tom May, nephew, I believe, of Henry May.

Doctor Wood had his office and drug store where Bishop & Co.'s bank now is, at the corner of Merchant and Kaahumanu streets. Dr. Hoffman was his first clerk in his drug store. Dr. Wood had to take over Koloa plantation from the government in payment for money owing to him. Dr. Wood's residence was on Hotel street and was afterwards occupied by Dr. McGrew. It has since been knocked down to make room for the Young hotel. For a long time it was one of the best houses in Honolulu. It was built by a firm called Bent, McKeen and Paterson. I helped to finish it. Dr. Wood was called by the natives "Kauka po alo maka" on account of having taken out a native's eyeball during some operation and then returned it to the socket. Originally the house was a one-story coral building, but it was afterwards raised to two stories. While the work was in progress, I remember an accident happening to a little half-white boy, son of Albert Robinson, foreman on the job. The boy was playing underneath, when a small crowbar was accidentally dropped from an upper story. It went through the boy's skull and out at his lower jaw. Miraculously enough, the boy recovered, and in later years was mail carrier between Honolulu and Koolau.

Henry Sea was an Englishman and jailor at the fort, Honolulu. Later on was partner with John Sumner, the original owner of Sumner's island in Honolulu harbor, now about dredged away. This John Sumner was the father of the present John Sumner and now an old man, in 1909, and still living in Honolulu. Henry Sea and old Sumner had both of them houses in what is now called Palace yard. Sumner's house was about where the Richard street entrance to the Palace grounds is and Sea's was further mauka. I helped to build Sumner's house.

ALEXANDER ADAMS AND THE HAWAIIAN FLAG

One of my earliest acquaintances in Honolulu was Captain Alexander Adams, an old Scotch skipper, who was formerly one of the pilots at Honolulu harbor. At the date of my arrival at Honolulu, he had retired from active life, and was then living at his ease. He was then 68 years old. His son, Alexander Adams II., succeeded him as pilot. I have several times heard old Alec tell the story of how the Hawaiian flag was designed by himself. Adams was married to a chiefess, and was employed by Kamehameha in positions of trust where sea matters were concerned. Kamehameha, who wished to trade on his own account, had already sent a vessel to China laden with sandal wood, but it was seized at Macao. The king then proposed to Captain Adams that he go to Canton in charge of a second vessel laden with the same kind of cargo. Adams, who was an old man-o'-war's man, said to the king, "If I go, I want a flag and a regular commission." The king and his councillors consulted among themselves, and afterwards, Adams explained to them the necessity for a national flag and ship's papers, else the vessel would be liable to be confiscated as a pirate. They consented to his request and placed the matter of designing a flag in his hands. Adams went home and drew a pattern of a flag to scale. He placed the British Union Jack in the canton, as at that time, Kamehameha used to hoist a British flag, he having ceded the islands, or at least the island of Hawaii, to Vancouver in 1794, and apparently ever since had seemed to consider himself under the protection of Britain. Then for the fly of the flag, Adams drew stripes colored alternately red, white and blue, to represent the principal islands of the group. He got his native wife to set her women to make a flag of tapa according to this pattern, and after it was finished, he submitted same to Kamehameha and the chiefs, who approved of it. From the sample flag made by the women servants of Mrs. Adams, a regular flag was made of the usual bunting, and this was flown by Captain Adams when he made this trip to Canton, and was the occasion when the Hawaiian flag was first flown to the breeze. Not only have I heard Captain Adams tell this account of the making of the flag to myself, but I have heard him repeat the same to the captains of several British men-o'-war who touched at Honolulu. Captain Harbottle, who worked as pilot about the same time as Captain Adams, also confirmed the foregoing to me. I was told the same story of the designing of the flag by Tom Phillips, who, when I arrived at Lahaina in 1844, had been a resident at Lahaina for a great many years. Ap Jones, who was a police magistrate at Lahaina and an old resident on the islands, corroborated Phillips. During the sixty-five years that I have resided in these islands, I have never heard any other name but that of Alexander Adams mentioned in connection with the designing of the flag. It was the common talk in Honolulu that he had designed it. Captain Adams kept a journal in which he jotted down various happenings of interest and this was recorded in it. The journal is still in existence in the possession of Mary Adams, a daughter. From time to time this diary has been lent to various parties to make extracts therefrom, and the last time I saw it I noticed that several pages had been torn out of it. Before his death, Captain Adams published a pamphlet giving an account of some of the events in his life, but I have never seen a copy.

Captain Adams lived out at Kalihi most of the time, although he had a house in town in what was known as Adams Lane. The grounds at Kalihi were known as Adams Gardens. They afterwards came into the possession of Allen Herbert and he, I think, sold the premises to the Alexander Young Hotel to be used as a dairy farm. The first mango tree ever planted in the Hawaiian islands is growing on this property. One day, Captain Adams, when he went outside to bring into the harbor a vessel hailing from Canton, noticed some mango seeds lying on the deck. Knowing what they were, he put them in his pocket and afterwards planted them at his place at Kalihi. One of the seeds sprouted and grew up. The first crop consisted of five mangos, and the seeds of these were again planted and from these trees were propagated most of the mango trees now found all over the islands.

One of Captain Adams bosom friends was Andrew Auld, like himself hailing from north of the Tweed. He was a wheelwright, and had his adobe-built shop on Beretania street, about opposite General Miller's house. For forty years these two used to dine together on Sundays. On one occasion only was this custom nearly interrupted. One Sunday, both having been indulging in a little too much mountain dew, they began arguing about something or other, and they both got so excited that at last Captain Adams ordered Auld to get out of his house and never show his face there again. Next Sunday when dinner time arrived and no Andrew turned up, Captain Adams wonderingly enquired what had become of "Andrew." His folks reminded him that he had ordered him out of the house on the previous Sunday. The old man, who had apparently forgot all about the incident, then shouted out in stentorian quarter-deck tones, "All hands on deck." "Go and fetch him right away, as soon as you can. Captain Adams' son, William, married Mary, daughter of Andrew Auld.

Captain Adams died in 1871 aged 91 years, and lies buried in Nuuanu Cemetery in the same grave with his old cronie, Andrew Auld. The flat gravestone which marks their common grave reads as follows:

Alexander Adams	Andrew Auld
a native of	a native of
Arbroth (sic), Forfarshire,	Linlithgow, Scotland,
Scotland	Born Sept. 8, 1799,
Born Dec. 27, 1780,	Died Oct. 26, 1873.
Died Oct. 27, 1871	

And at the foot of the stone is the couplet:
"Twa croanies frae the land of heather,
Are sleepin' here in death th'gether."

Judge Abraham Fornander had a high opinion of Captain Adams and he speaks of him and Young and Davis in the Sandwich Islands Magazine which appeared in 1856.

Charles R. Bishop.—Remember when he arrived. He started a small dry goods store on the S. E. corner of Maunakea and King

15

Streets. There were eleven partners in the partnership, and the firm name was Coday, Calhoun, Bishop & Co. Coday married Jim Robinson's daughter by his first wife. Robinson afterwards set up Coday on his own hook. The match between C. R. Bishop and Bernice Pauahi was a runaway one. They were married on Hawaii, without the consent of Paki, who, however, forgave them.

Charles Brewer I.—Was well acquainted with him. Last time I met him was when he asked me on board the "Nettie Merrill" to have mid-day lunch with him. Brewer was a small but rather well built man. Fair and pleasant to do business with. C. Brewer I started business on Kaahumanu Street, about where Morgan's auction room now is. Charles Brewer II was in business at the same time, but on the opposite side of the street and a little farther makai. They were both ship chandlers and commission merchants.

Captain Carter.—I cannot recall his face, but of course knew all his sons, Sam, Henry, Joe, who died recently, and H. A. P. or "Happy," as he was called.

Isaac Montgomery and his brother Dan had a store in a two-story coral building standing on the makai waikiki side of King and Maunakea Streets. Isaac had left the islands before I came to the islands, but I saw him in California. Once saw him putting $40,000 on monte table one night and lose it all. This was in the Shades, one of the leading gambling hells in San Francisco. Whilst in San Francisco I visited both the Shades and the El Dorado, both gambling places, but I never speculated myself, merely went as a spectator. Dan, the younger brother, was sent down to Puuloa to manage the salt works there. Later on he went to Kailua, Hawaii, where he was when I rebuilt the native Protestant church. Isaac returned to the islands and settled here. At their death they left all their money to the R. C. Church.

James Austen, partner in Austen and Beccles. Kept a dry goods store on the S. E. corner of King and Nuuanu streets. A son of Austen married a daughter of George Woods, and later on she married John D. Holt.

Jim Smith, father of the late Jim Smith, of the Board of Education, of Mrs. John Sullivan, Mrs. Hassinger and Mrs. George Ross, was a school teacher. He came up to Honolulu from Tahiti. Had a school of his own. Jim Smith married the adopted daughter of a missionary in Tahiti.

James Robinson, who along with his partner Robert Lawrence did a big business at the "old point" where Allen & Robin-

16

son's lumber yard is. James or Jimmie Robinson was a ship's carpenter, a native of Deptford, England, and Robert (Bobbie) Lawrence was, I think, a ship's cooper. They were shipwrecked on what was afterwards called the Pearl and Hermes Reef to the N.W. of these islands. The crews of the wrecked vessels managed to construct boats out of the wrecks, and ultimately reached Honolulu. Robinson & Lawrence started a business in Honolulu as shipwrights. Had about 50 or 60 men in their employment. They had arrived in the islands before me. Mark, Jimmie's son, has a good deal of resemblance to Jimmie, but Jimmie was not so tall. He was a good business man, and you had to toe the mark when working for him. Work hours were the same as at Lahaina, viz., from sunrise to sunset, and the wages $2 per day. About the time I arrived in Honolulu in 1848, his workmen struck for shorter hours. They wanted from 6 to 6 and from 6 to 4 on Saturdays. They gained their point. Bobbie Lawrence used to look after the grog shop which the firm had in the yard, and which stood about the same place where Sam Dwight has a small office. Bobbie was already an old man when I knew him. Last job I did for Jimmie was helping to move a shed in his yard. The old coral building in the yard with the ship's figurehead on the makai side, was where the firm kept their supply of timber, oakum, etc. Instead of felt to put underneath the ship's copper, Robinson used to buy bales of tapa from the government, which had been received in taxes. All tapas, pigs etc., received by the government in payment of taxes were stored in a yard on Nuuanu Street, where Mrs. Foster's building now is on the mauka side of Marine Street. This yard was enclosed by a wooden fence, and inside was a wooden shed where the tapas were stored. Robinson would buy 50 bales of tapa at a time. I used to buy tapas myself, usually sold by the "book" or set of five. The cost was $1.25 for the book, or 25c each. I used them for blankets and continued to do so for a good many years after I came to the islands. So did many of the other white residents. When they got dirty they were thrown away and a new set bought.

The ship's figurehead on the front of the old coral building in Allen & Robinson's yard was got off the ship London, wrecked on the island of Lanai. Robinson bought the wreck and brought down the figurehead and stuck it up where it now is. The figure head represents Alderman Wood, Lord Mayor of London, celebrated as the champion of Queen Caroline, wife of George IV.

I remember old Jimmie showing me a doctor's bill he had just received. He said, "Look here, matey, that's putting it on. They think they can put it on because Jim Robinson's well off, but they don't know how many mouths I've got to feed." It was a bill of Dr. McKibbin (father of Dr. R. McKibbin and Alec McKibbin) for $29 for vaccinating two children. Robinson originally got his land on the water front by a deed signed by Kalaimoku, one of Kamehameha's warriors. It was afterwards claimed by one of the kings, and Robinson had to undergo a long and expensive lawsuit to defend his title to the place, same costing him about $47,000. Even after this, I remember a native soldier being sent by Kamehameha III requesting Robinson to stop building a new shed or building within the yard. Jimmie said to the soldier, "Tell that damned n----- king, I'll put up the house in spite of him. I've spent $47,000 already and can afford to spend another $40,000."

Doctor Robert McKibbin was the father of the late Dr. Robert McKibbin and of Alexander McKibbin, still living on Maui. He had his surgery and drug store on Queen street, opposite Brewer & Co. After his death, his two sons succeeded him, Robert as doctor and Alec in charge of the drug store.

Paddy Montgomery was uncle to Robert and Alec McKibbin, and was a lawyer. They made him police judge to keep him out of mischief.

Henry S. Swinton was a Scotchman. Deputy Governor of Maui and a little tin god in Lahaina. Was head of the Customs there and a regular Poo Bah. Later on came to live in Honolulu. Harry Swinton, living in Honolulu, is his son. His daughter married Captain John Brown, jailor, Oahu prison. This Brown, before becoming jailor, was bookkeeper for Charlie Vincent, carpenter and builder. Before Captain Brown, a Mickey Brown held the same job.

Henry Cooper was clerk with Starkey & Janion. Came from England on purpose. Died at Kaawaloa, Kona. His widow still here. Two sons were with W. G. Irwin & Co. and another son is bookkeeper at Hana, Maui.

Billy Irwin's father was a bookkeeper for Starkey & Janion, but was discharged by that firm. The father was here in 1848. Mother started a boarding house for a living. Remember Billy as a boy playing baseball on what is called the Esplanade. First job he got was with Lewers & Dickson. Afterwards was a clerk in the postoffice.

18

Joe Booth was a Sydney duck. Knew him well. Father of Charlie Booth. Was married to a native wife, but got rid of her and then re-married. Kept a grog shop which was called "Paulo Parade." Joe called his place "The Blonde," but the original Blonde grog shop or hotel was on Bethel street. Booth's place was situated a little to the rear of the southwest corner of Nuuanu and King streets, behind the two-story coral building now standing.

Thomas Pratt formerly of Honolulu. Knew him at Koloa, Kauai, where he kept a small store and boarding house for plantation employees.

William Maxwell, steward on a ship to Australia. Afterwards butcher, Honolulu. Half white descendants here.

James Mahoney worked for Jimmie Robinson. Lived at Kalihi near Captain Adams' place.

Captain William Paty was skipper of the Yankee, running between Honolulu and San Francisco. Made over 100 passages He was father of the late John A. Paty of Bishop & Co. and Mrs. Mott Smith. I have in my possession an old koa table which once belonged to Captain Paty. Was made by Fisher, cabinetmaker. Captain Paty paid $75 for it. The wood is as sound today as when the table was made. It is made of the mountain koa which is not so subject to the attacks from worms like the koa grown lower down. Strangers coming to Honolulu would sometimes ask the way to Captain Paty's house in Nuuanu valley, and they would be informed, "Go right ahead till you come to the first shower, then turn to the right."

William Jarrett was an Englishman. Acted as a sort of secretary to Dr. Judd, who was then the little king of the islands. Jarrett arrived here as master-at-arms on board one of the vessels of Wilkes Expedition, and after getting his discharge at Honolulu on October 31, 1840, settled here for the remainder of his life. He was the grandfather of the present sheriff of Honolulu. Old Bill first of all lived out on the plains, beyond Atherton's house on King street, and afterwards shifted in to town on what is now the extension of Vineyard street, between Fort and Nuuanu streets. He died of dropsy.

William Ladd and John Ladd had a hardware store and commission agency. They went to California in 1849. The late J. O. Carter was married to a daughter of one of them. Makai of J. O. Carter's premises on Nuuanu street is the Ladd place.

19

A. S. Cleghorn came from New Zealand with his father and two brothers. I was settled on Kauai when they arrived. Old Cleghorn started a store (dry goods) on Nuuanu street at place where a Chinese keeps hardware store, between King and Hotel. Cleghorn came here about 1854. Remember A. S. Cleghorn as a boy. Remember coming to Honolulu from Kauai with wife the same month that Kamehameha III died. Wife bought some things, including two silk handkerchiefs at Cleghorn's store. Came home and found the handkerchiefs weren't in the parcel. Went back. Cleghorn swore he put them in. Got no satisfaction.

F. W. Thompson was an auctioneer. Was going to marry one of Dr. Judd's daughters. Committed suicide.

Edward C. Webster great man for horse racing. Was connected with Henry Macfarlane of the Commercial Saloon.

Stephen Reynolds. Knew him well. Was a little, short, dried up sort of man. Storekeeper and acted as North German or Bremen consul. Had his consulate on Nuuanu street, entering from a lane, mauka of the Royal Saloon. Ran a school for half-white girls on Union lane, one of the earliest on the islands. Harry Sheldon's wife and his sister, Angeline, were educated there; also C. B. Wilson's wife's mother and Ned Bush's sister.

John Meek was pilot when I came here. Used to live on King street where Smith street now is. Horace Crabbe married his daughter. Meek was a good kind of fellow. High Mason. Was a well built, compact man.

Pilot Archie McIntyre was captain of a ship and brother of old Hugh McIntyre (father of present Hugh). He came to the islands after my arrival here.

John Needles lived in a grass hut on a lane off Bethel street in rear of Houghtailing's house. He was of mixed blood. Had two sons, one a cripple, the other a carpenter who died at Hilo.

Brickwood was a midshipman on the first man-o'-war steamship which sailed from Plymouth, England. I remember seeing it steam out of Plymouth and reminded Brickwood of the event. Brickwood later on became a lieutenant. He was appointed to take charge of Honolulu fort and afterwards became postmaster, Honolulu.

John R. Von Pfister, knew him by sight. Think he died abroad. Related to Godfrey and the other Browns.

James Campbell, millionaire. Came to the islands about February, 1850. First met him at Koloa, Kauai, where Campbell, Turton and a man named Rose came along on the tramp looking for work. He was a ship's carpenter by trade. I was then working at Koloa, but was unable to give Campbell work. In after years, when I was working upon some repair job at Campbell's Emma street house, I reminded Campbell of this incident on Kauai. He remembered it, but of course could not recall my face. Jim Campbell, father of Princess Kawananakoa, Mrs. Shingle, Mrs. Walter Macfarlane and Mrs. Beckley.

Louis Gravier was a Frenchman. Had a store on Nuuanu street, near Joe Booth's "Blonde," and another on King street near Friel's grog shop, about where Yee Hop's butcher shop is now situated. Blew out his brains.

Chinese. There were not many in the country when I came here. A few storekeepers, servants, and a few working on the newly started sugar plantations. No Japanese, Koreans, Filippinos some Portuguese| There were a few of the last mentioned, who had come here on whaleships. About a dozen Chinamen in Honolulu. Principal Chinese storekeeper was Sam Sing, whose store was on Fort street, where the Hawaiian Trust Company's building has been built.

William Wood and George Wood were two brothers who did a sort of "kuleana" grabbing business. Had store on Nuuanu street, opposite "old corner." Sold dry goods. At that time there was a building that stood at the foot of Nuuanu street causing the street to branch out into two. I forget what this building that stood in the middle of Nuuanu street was originally erected for. Later on Rodanet (afterwards a watchmaker and sugar boiler) kept a coffee shop there. Above Wood's store on corner of Nuuanu street, the French consul had his office.

Charity School. The top of the old Charity school was moved to Likelike street and formed part of Pohukaina school. Wiggins & Lucas had the contract. Close to the Charity school on the site of Aliiolani Hale was Judge Ii's house.

Hudson's Bay Company was just giving up business when I came to Honolulu.

Grandfather of Kalakaua, Likelike and Liliuokalani was hanged for killing his wife.

Kalakaua had a negro face and curly, frizzy hair. As a boy used to run around barefoot. Half-brother of Kalakaua lives at Koolau.

21

Two-story wooden house which used to be where the Harrison block is now on corner of Beretania and Fort streets, was imported from Boston and was intended to be put on top of the one-story adobe house occupied by General Miller. It was feared that it would be too heavy for that place and was erected instead on Beretania and Fort streets.

Hawaiian Band. The first Hawaiian Band belonged to Kamehameha III. About two dozen performers. Two or three of them were North American Indians, Oliver being one of them, and the balance were negroes. Black George was the principal player. I don't know how these negroes had turned up in Honolulu. Perhaps some of them had served on ships as cooks or in some other capacity. Merseburg was the first bandmaster. The first public performance took place in old Royal Hawaiian Theater, corner of Alakea and Hotel streets, where the Masonic Temple now is. Merseburg had two sons and two daughters, one of them being the young girl who was spirited away by . . . on board the yacht . . . W. C. Parke gives an account of it in his printed reminiscences.

Games and old Honolulu. When I first came to Honolulu there were very few games played by the boys. The missionaries had frowned upon surf swimming and other ancient Hawaiian amusements and nothing had taken their place. Boys used to be very fond of lassooing each other. For the white sailorman or mechanics, the only thing to do was to frequent a "grog shop" or a "whore shop." Tobacco and cigars were cheaper then than nowadays. Cigars, $1 per 100. Fish was cheap. The first Honolulu fish market was where the Metropolitan Meat Market is on King street, and right across the street where Dimond's store is, was another small fish market. Next to the fish market on Dimond's side of the street, stood an adobe house where Bill Brash, now living on Emma street, was born.

Duke of Edinburgh. I remember his visit to Honolulu. Remember seeing him and Lord Charles Beresford in Bennett's bookstore on Fort street. This store was afterwards occupied by Smith, son of Rev. Mr. Smith. Bennett cleared out for the States with a troupe of hula girls. The house where the Duke of Edinburgh lived when in Honolulu was still standing until a year or two ago at the back of the old Court House, now occupied by H. Hackfeld & Co. The house faced on what was afterwards known as Edinburgh street. It was originally built for Governor

Kekuanaoa, but was fitted up for the reception of the Duke. I helped to put up a makai verandah on the house. The father of Jim Torbert, formerly with the Pacific Hardware Company, was head carpenter on the job.

Fowler's Yard belonged first to a painter called "Putty Wright." Big Stewart, husband of Mrs. Stewart, School street, and father of Mrs. T. Lloyd and Stewart, Koolau, worked for Putty Wright. Stewart came here from the Colonies.

John de Fries, father of Henry and John de Fries, was a rough carpenter, married to a native from Mahukona. Became a Mormon and went to Salt Lake. His wife became crazy.

Rev. Daniel Dole. Knew him when head of the Punahou school. I did repair work at Punahou during his time. His son, now Judge Stanford B. Dole, was then a small boy playing around the school yard.

First Fire Engine. First time that a fire engine was used in Honolulu was at a fire that broke out on premises at corner of Maunakea and King streets. In those days there was no regular supply of water laid in pipes throughout the town. Wells were the only supply. The excitement caused by the fire and the using of the new machine was so great that, by mistake, the suction pipe was laid down a cesspool in the supposition that it was a well. When pumping began, the foreman, Gill, received the contents of the cesspool over his face and body.

Kalakaua, Makaeha and Likelike used to live in a small one-story, wooden building, situated about where the Kapiolani building now is on Alakea and King streets. This building was not in existence when I first came to Honolulu, but on my return to Honolulu from Kauai, it had been built.

KAUAI

Went to Kauai February 17, 1850, to build a scow for George Charman. Took a contract to build a schooner at Kipu, up Niumalu river for a native. Got the ribs up when the native died and lost all my work. Took another contract to build a schooner for Paul Kanoa (old Paul). Built and finished it. Paul Kanoa took two years to pay for it. In the intervals, while waiting for lumber to finish this schooner, Widemann came over and I went to Lihue and built the first wooden house there. Went to work permanently on the plantation. Wages for plantation laborers were $12\frac{1}{2}$ cents per day in paper money. This paper money was worth at other stores outside the plantation but 6 1-4 cents. The different storekeepers would exchange their paper money from time to time at par.

One morning woke up and found I had a stroke of paralysis. J. F. B. Marshall was then at Lihue. He was one of the chief shareholders and the real manager. He acted as the medical man on the plantation. They sent off to Koloa for Dr. Smith, W. O. Smith's father. On his arrival, a mirror was placed at my mouth—no signs of life and pronounced dead. They made a box for a coffin and I was just being lifted into it when my chum, Kasang, who was holding my head, noticed a quiver on one of my eyelids. Marshall got busy with me and by and bye I was able to speak. After two weeks could stand, but unable to walk. Took passage in a little schooner from Hanamaulu bay for Honolulu. Took eleven days to get as far as off Waianae. There becalmed and hired a native canoe for $3 to take me to Honolulu, but the breeze sprang up, and as we were coming into Honolulu harbor, the schooner arrived a little ahead of the canoe. Was carried up to Dr. Newcombe's who lived opposite old Kaumakapili church. Dr. Hillebrand was there at the same time under treatment. Remained there for two or three weeks. Got better very suddenly. Dr. Newcombe said I couldn't live a year. I said: "Doctor, I won't die to suit you. I'll see you damned first." I got up out of bed and walked straight out of his house. I then went to live in a house where afterwards was situated Fowler's Yard, and was nursed by Mrs. Stewart, who afterwards lived for a great many years on School street, near Fort.

Returned to Lihue Plantation, but left there at the same time as my mate, Henry Kasang, a native of New York and a boat builder by trade.

After leaving Lihue I took a contract from Dr. Judd to build the first court house on the bluff at Nawiliwili, and also a story and a half house for Paul Kanoa at Niumalu under the bluff. Then went to work for W. H. Pease, cane planter between Lihue and Haupuu, towards the kukui grove. Pease would go away from the place for a long time, and I had to sell a horse to buy poi and food for myself and for Pease's boys, who were starving. Had to sue Pease for my wages. J. F. B. Marshall and E. P. Bond acted as arbitrators in the case and they decided in my favor. I got married to a native woman at Nawiliwili by Judge Bond. Got the license from Kekuanaoa when on a visit to Honolulu.

Afterwards went to Koloa, then a straggling place. Tobey

plantation still going. George Gilmore, manager, in partnership with Stephen Reynolds. Burnham had been manager of Koloa plantation, but had just left. Morse was manager when I went there. Peck had a small plantation at Maunakilika, but had just left. He was the man who backed Titcomb in his silk venture. Went to work at Koloa plantation. After working for ten months couldn't get any money or settlement from Burbank, who had become manager and half-interest partner with Dr. Wood. I went to Judge Bond and he advised me to put the case to arbitration. J. F. B. Marshall represented me and Zenas Bent represented Judge Burbank. Won the case but still couldn't get any coin, so took out attachment in the native magistrate's court (Lilikalani, magistrate), and then Burbank came to the scratch, after the judge had sent a police constable to levy on the mill. This police constable, by the bye, was a native by the name of Kanihoomole, a poor worthless wretch. His sister was married to this Judge Lilikalani, and the E. Lilikalani who lives in Honolulu and poses as a chief, is named after this judge and is a son of Kanihoomole. I remember when E. Lilikalani was born. He is no more a chief than I am.

Bob Brown was then blacksmith at Koloa. In after years he lived at Kaneohe, Koolau, and on dying a few years ago made me his heir. He left me several thousand dollars. He was a native of Richmond, England, and came to the islands about 1839. Brown was a great eater in those days at Koloa. Most of the white men working on the plantation boarded at Tom Pratt's. Pratt usually fried three eggs each morning for each boarder's breakfast. There were about six of us boarders, and we resolved to put up a job on Bob Brown. So one morning, just when the big platter of fried eggs was served, all hands pretended to become deeply engaged in an argument about something or other, meanwhile neglecting to touch their breakfast. While the argument was in progress, Brown never said a word, but was tucking into the eggs. After finishing his own he continued helping himself from the dish, until he had scoffed the whole lot. Just when Brown was finishing the last egg the company suddenly ceased their conversation and burst out laughing. Brown looked up and saw they were enjoying a joke at his expense, and immediately jumped up and ran out of the house. He never boarded at Pratt's after that, and, in fact, kept himself a hermit as long as he remained at Koloa.

After working for the plantation I set up for myself in Koloa as a carpenter and wheelwright, and stayed there until 1859, when I went over to Hanalei to build a schooner. I bought some land on the flat near the mouth of the river, started a store and began planting cane. I bought twelve and one-half acres from Henry Rhodes, brother of Godfrey Rhodes, for $50 an acre, and it cost $30 an acre more to clear. Planted it in Lahaina cane and got five tons sugar to an acre the first crop. This was the first occasion on the islands when they got five tons sugar per acre. Everyone had laughed at me for planting cane there. Fred Wundenberg, father of Fred Wundenberg, postmaster general, Honolulu, was then the manager of Hanalei or Princeville plantation. Old Wundenberg was married to a Miss Henry, a daughter or granddaughter of one of the first lot of English missionaries that came out to Tahiti from England in the ship Duff.

My house was near the mouth of the river. In addition to storekeeping and cane planting I carried on the business of wheelwright. Got into difficulties through advancing money to Jack Markle. Went to Honolulu with my books. Showed that I was worth $32,000 with good stock of goods. E. O. Hall was my principal creditor. Assigned my property, including cane land and crops. Latter was sold off at a sacrifice. I subsequently secured 85 acres at Hanalei mauka, where I built a house and grew cane for sale to the plantation. I lived there until my wife died, when I sold out and came back to Honolulu.

R. C. Wyllie had become the owner of Hanalei plantation and he put in John Low, father of Eben and John Low, etc., to be manager. John Low had been mate of a ship and got ashore at Hawaii, where he worked for some time on a plantation under Willfong. He was about five feet eight inches, stout and good looking. Was no manager and didn't know how to control the native labor, who worked just as they pleased. Got the plantation into debt. I was there when R. C. Wyllie's nephew committed suicide. After old Wyllie died, he left twelve administrators of his estate, and John Low as manager of the plantation. Old Wyllie's nephew went down to the plantation to stay, and shortly after he got there, asked the manager for the plantation books in order to look them over. He got them, and on Low returning to the office after an absence of two hours or so, young Wyllie pitched the books out at the window, saying, "Here, Low, your books are like yourself, not worth a damn."

I remember well the evening when young Wyllie did away

26

with himself. A party of the white men were at Low's house where we had some music on the fiddle, concertina, etc., several of the men being good performers of dance music. In the interval, Low went off to get some limes to make lemonade, and Wyllie went out of the room to fetch a jug of water. Low returned with the limes, but Wyllie did not make his reappearance. After waiting some time, Low said, "Where's Wyllie, we must find him. He's been off his head for some weeks." We searched the house and at last, on opening the door of a large privy situated outside, Wyllie fell forward into the arms of Low, the blood gushing from a wound in his throat, which he had cut with a razor. We carried him to the house and tried to sew up the wound, stanching it with cotton. The plantation blacksmith, Henry Smith (father of Henry Smith, clerk of the Supreme Court) made a canula out of Mexican dollars, which we inserted into his throat. Wyllie recovered consciousness. A whaleboat was dispatched to Honolulu for Dr. McKibbin, but Wyllie died before he arrived. Wyllie, before dying, became perfectly sensible and asked for a pencil and paper. He wrote: "Oh! my poor mother, don't tell mother. Fix it up so she won't know." Low asked who was to get the property. He wrote: "All for mother." Low said, "Wont you give Ada anything." (Ada von Pfister, to whom he was engaged.) He wrote: "One half." Wyllie's uncle, Mr. Macdonald, came out from Scotland to settle up the estate, which turned out to be heavily in debt. The whole of R. C. Wyllie's estate on Kauai and in Honolulu was sold off and was sacrificed. We on the plantation had to get up a subscription to help pay Mr. Macdonald's expenses back home.

John Kellett, father of Danson Kellett, lived on the bluff at Hanalei, overlooking the valley. His house was a large, long, one-storied building, and is still standing, being now occupied by Japanese. Kellett acted as pilot at Hanalei. A lot of land at Hanalei was owned by him. He used to make butter, etc. The so-called Russian fort near the point at Hanalei was never finished, only the foundations were built. It was never so far advanced as the fort at Waimea. People going from Hanalei to Waimea or Hanapepe would use the mountain trail. This must be pretty much the same route as is taken by the electric power line from Wainiha to Eleele.

Remember Kamehameha IV and Queen Emma calling at my store in Hanalei. First thing they asked for was a drink of okolehao, which Jack Markle used to manufacture. Remember swimming in Haena caves. Party from an English man-o'-war visited the caves while I was there. They got a gig up from the ship and the natives had two canoes. The gig, when launched, was being dragged under the roof of the cave by a current and had to be brought back by the help of the natives in their canoes. The water in the cave would be clear, then a scum would cover the face of the water and then it would sink. Scores of times I've seen the natives throwing down the burning brands from Haena heights.

Charlie Titcomb sold his land in Hanalei to Wyllie and bought land at Kilauea, where he induced some parties to start in planting cane.

I have never seen the volcano, although I have worked at Hilo for ten months at a stretch. The nearest I have been to the volcano has been the 11-mile house.

I left Hanalei in 1868, and with the proceeds of 25 acres cane, horses, cattle, etc., I came to Honolulu with the intention of taking a trip to England and seeing my folks there. I put my daughter in school and paid for two years tuition in advance. I was staying at Currie's boarding house on Maunakea street, and had all my money with me. On awakening one day from a sleep I found that all my money was stolen. I informed the police, and all the satisfaction I got was that if I could point out the thief they would arrest him. I had consequently to put off my trip and go back to work at the jack plane. I have never been back to England since I left it.

Acknowledgements & Thanks

Thrums Hawaiian Annual

Hawaiian Historical Society

Hawaii State Archives

Hawaii State Library

Barry Lawrence Ruderman Antique Maps, Inc.

Paul Emmert

Newspapers.com

Don Hibbard

Linda Sueyoshi

Gary R. Coover – Annotator

An award-winning author and researcher, Gary created a walking tour and virtual marker program that won a Preservation Award from Preservation Arkansas, and his history of Honolulu's Chinatown buildings recently won a Preservation Award from the Historic Hawaii Foundation.

Now living in Honolulu, Gary has researched building histories for over 30 years and has identified architects, builders, and construction dates for well over a thousand buildings in Texas, Arkansas, and Hawaii.

Featured on HGTV's "Dream Drives" and "If Walls Could Talk" television programs, Gary was also a presenter for the popular Historic Neighborhoods lecture series at the Rice University School of Continuing Studies in Houston, Texas.

Other works by Gary include *Honolulu Chinatown: 200 Years of Red Lanterns & Red Lights* (2022), *Pocket Walking Tour of Honolulu's Chinatown* (2023), *Downtown Honolulu's Lost Buildings and Forgotten Architects* (2023), and *Honolulu 1854: The Drawings of Paul Emmert*, published by Rollston Press.

INDEX

Adams, Alexander, 33, 69
Admiral Thomas, 25
Akamai, 72
Armstrong, Richard, 56, 58
Armstrong, Samuel C., 56, 58
Atherton, C.H., 24
Austin, James V., 20
Bishop, Bernice Pauahi, 35, 46, 50
Bishop, Charles R., 35, 50
Blonde, The, 9, 41, 68
Bolles, Benjamin F., 75
Booth, Joe, 9, 68
Brannan, Sam, 31
Brewer, Charles, 29, 70, 78
Brinsmade, Peter, 6, 69, 70, 74
Brown, George, 32
Brown, J.H., 35
Bungalow, The, 37
Carter, J.O., 54
Central Union church, 38
Charlton, Richard, 42
Colcord, John, 29
Commercial Hotel, 53
Cooke, A.S., 49, 51
Cummings, Thomas, 69
Cummins, John, 25
Damon, Father, 30, 65, 66
Davis, Robert L., 26, 71
Dimond, Henry, 40
Dole, Rev. Daniel, 5, 42
Dominis, Capt. John O., 27
Dominis, Captain John O., 32, 57
Dowsett, Mrs., 32
Dudoit, Jules, 39
E. O. Hall & Son, Ltd., 45
French Hotel, 27
French, William, 18, 36
Gilman & Co., 76, 77
Gilman Brothers, 77
Globe Hotel, 45

Gloucester, 5, 61
Goodale, Warren, 78
Grimes, Eliab, 8, 68
Haalelea, 38
Hall, E.O., 25
Hildebrand, Dr., 26
Holmes, Hannah, 44
Holt, Robert, 19, 20
Honolulu Fort, 20
Honolulu Library & Reading Room, 34
Hooper, William, 6, 62
Hudson's Bay Company, 8, 9, 33, 68
Hunnewell, James L., 26, 78
Iolani Palace, 47
James Robinson & Co., 19
Jarves, James Jackson, 33, 34
Johnny Wright's shipyard, 62
Johnstone, A., 24
Jones, Eli, 54
Judd, Dr. G.P., 22, 48
Kaeo, 38
Kalakaua, David, 50
Kamehameha III, 34, 48, 49, 65
Kamehameha IV, 35, 41, 47, 50
Kamehameha V, 37, 50
Kanaina, 48
Kaumakapili Church, 52
Kawaiahao Church, 40, 58, 78
Kealiiahonui, 23
Kekauluohi, 48
Kekauonohi, 23
Kekuanoa, 23, 49, 62
Kilimana, 74
Kinau, 49
Konia, 46
Ladd & Co., 6, 7, 16, 62, 68, 69, 74

Ladd, William, 69
Lahilahi, 38
Lawrence, Robert, 19
Lee, Chief Justice, 72
Lewers & Cooke, 25
Little Britain, 24
Lunalilo, 48, 50
Makiki, 24
Manini, 7, 62
Manuahi, 8, 68
Mauna Kilika, 23
Meek, Capt. John, 41, 69
Miller, General William, 55
Montgomery, Isaac, 41, 69
Moses, 49, 51
Mott-Smith, Dr., 26
Newell, Capt., 32
Nicholson, Charles H., 43
Oahu Charity School, 24
Odd Fellows, 33, 41, 45, 69
Pakaka, 19
Paki, 46
Parke, William C., 33, 71
Paty, Captain John, 69
Paty, John & William, 16
Paty, William, 16, 55, 66
Paulet, Lord George, 21, 48, 51
Pelly, George, 9, 33, 68
Pierce & Brewer, 26
Piikoi, 46
Pitman, Benjamin, 78
Prince Lot, 37
Princess Victoria, 37, 50

Queen Emma, 12, 35, 50
Reynolds, Stephen, 6, 14, 16, 25, 41, 61, 63, 68
Richards, Rev. William, 46, 65
Ripley, C.B., 61
Robertson, Judge, 33
Robeson, Bobby, 21
Robinson, James, 19
Roman Catholic church, 28
Rooke, Dr. T.C.B., 12, 50, 53
Royal Hawaiian Theatre, 35
Sam Sing & Co., 25
Seamen's Bethel, 30, 42, 43
Shillaber, Theodore, 37
Silva, Anton, 45
Simpson, Alexander, 21
Skinner, Henry, 11, 21
Smith, Captain F.C., 75
Smith, James, 55
Smith, Rev. Lowell, 52
Snow, Benjamin F., 17
Sumner, William, 38
Terrill, Mr., 27
Vincent, Charley, 35
Webster, E.C., 25, 64
Weston, David M., 78
Wheeler, S.B., 72
Williams, S.H., 45
Wond, William, 34
Wood, Dr. R. W., 32
Wood, R.A.S., 71
Young Chiefs' School, 49